AGAINST THE CHRISTIANS

THE ARGUMENTS OF THE

EMPEROR JULIAN

AGAINST THE

CHRISTIANS

TO WHICH ARE ADDED EXTRACTS FROM THE OTHER
WORKS OF JULIAN RELATIVE TO THE CHRISTIANS

TRANSLATED FROM THE GREEK FRAGMENTS
PRESERVED BY CYRIL, BISHOP OF ALEXANDRIA BY

THOMAS TAYLOR

THE KNOWLEDGE OF THE GODS IS VIRTUE, WISDOM, AND
PERFECT FELICITY, AND MAKES US RESEMBLE THE GODS.
- JAMBLICHUS

Originally published in 1809.

The layout, design, and cover art of this edition
copyright 2018, Gregory K. Koon.

Image of coin bearing Julian's likeness
used with the permission of
Classical Numismatic Group, Inc.
http://www.cngcoins.com

ISBN-13: 978-1987447859
ISBN-10: 1987447859

PREFACE

I REJOICE in the opportunity which is now afforded me of printing this translation of the extracts from a lost work* of Julian against the Christians; conceiving that it may be the means of benefitting *a certain few*, who though they have been educated in *stupid opinions*, have abandoned them, and who, if properly instructed in, would immediately embrace the genuine religion of mankind.

As man is naturally a religious animal, and as the *true* knowledge of divinity is, as Jamblichus beautifully observes, virtue, wisdom, and consummate felicity, nothing can be so important as the acquisition of this knowledge, and, as one of the means of obtaining it, a purification from theological error. Julian, who was certainly one of the most excellent emperors recorded in the annals of history, wrote, I am persuaded, the treatise from which these fragments are taken with no other view than to lead the reader of it to this most sublime knowledge, and the translator of these extracts can most solemnly affirm this was his only aim in translating and printing them.

A few copies only of this translation were printed, because a very few only in the present state of things are likely to be benefitted by it; and these few copies, for obvious reasons, are not published.

As an apology for certain *strong expressions* both in the fragments and accompanying notes, suffice it to say, that *false opinions in things of the greatest consequence cannot be too forcibly reprobated; and that those who are offended by these expressions are such as will never be*

---

* This work consisted of seven books.

purified from the errors they are intended to expose.

I, also, deem it necessary to observe, that Cyril, from whom these extracts are derived, is with the strongest reason suspected of being the cause of the murder of Hypatia, a lady who was one of the brightest ornaments of the Alexandrian school; who delivered instructions from that chair which Ammonius, Hierocles, and many other great philosophers had filled before, and who was not only a prodigy of learning, but also a paragon of beauty.

I shall only add, for the sake of the few who are capable of being benefitted by the perusal of these extracts, that the religion of the heathens, as promulgated by Orpheus, Pythagoras, Plato, and their followers, is founded on the following principles: That the cause of all things is perfectly simple, unindigent, and beneficent, and that in consequence of this he cannot be more fitly denominated than by the epithets of *the one* and *the good*; the former of these appellations denoting that all things proceed from him, and the latter that all things tend to him, as to the ultimate object of desire. That as it is necessary (the principle of things being *the one*) that the progression of beings should be continued, and that no vacuum should intervene either in incorporeal or corporeal natures; it is, also, necessary, that every thing which has a natural progression should proceed through similitude. That in consequence of this, it is necessary that every producing principle should generate a number of the same order with itself, viz. *nature*, a natural number; *soul*, one that is psychical (i.e. belonging to soul); and *intellect*, an intellectual number. For, if whatever possesses a power of generating generates similars prior to dissimilars, every cause must deliver its own form and characteristic property to its progeny; and before it generates that which gives subsistence to progressions far distant and separate from its nature, it must constitute things proximate to itself according to essence, and conjoined with it through similitude. It is, therefore, necessary from the preceding axioms, since there is one unity the principle of the universe, that this unity should produce from itself, prior to every thing else, a multitude of natures characterized by unity, and a number the most of all things allied to its cause; and these natures are no other than the gods.

No objections of any weight, no arguments but such as are sophistical, can be urged against this most sublime theory, which is so congenial to the unperverted conceptions of the human mind, that it can only be treated with ridicule and contempt in degraded, barren, and barbarous ages. Indolence and priestcraft, however, have hitherto conspired to defame those inestimable works,* in which this and many other sublime and important theories can alone be found; and the theology of the Greeks has been attacked with all the insane fury of ecclesiastical zeal, and all the imbecil flashes of mistaken wit, by men whose conceptions on the subject, like those of a man between sleeping and waking, have been turbid and wild, phantastic and confused, preposterous and vain.

THOMAS TAYLOR
1809

---

* viz. The works of Plotinus, Porphyry, Jamblichus, Syrianus, Proclus, Ammonius, Damascius, Olympiodorus, and Simplicius.

THE
ARGUMENTS
OF
THE EMPEROR JULIAN
AGAINST THE CHRISTIANS

IT appears to me to be proper that I should explain to all men the causes through which I am persuaded that the *fraudulent machination* of the Galilæans (σκευωρια) is the fiction of men, composed with an evil intention; and that it possesses indeed nothing divine, but employing that part of the soul which delights in the fabulous,which is puerile and stupid, adduces monstrous narrations in order to a belief of the truth.

But intending to speak of all their dogmas as they call them, I am desirous in the first place to observe, that it is requisite the reader, if he wishes to contradict what I assert, should, as in a court of justice, advance nothing foreign to the subject, nor, as it is said, recriminate till the first charges have been defended. For thus the proper subject of dispute will be in a better manner and more clearly determined, when he wishes to correct any thing that is advanced by us, and does not recriminate in answering what we consider to be reprehensible.

It is, however, worthwhile briefly to relate whence and how the conception of divinity first arrived to us. Afterwards, to compare what is said by the Greeks and the Hebrews of the divinity. And in the next place, to interrogate those who are neither Greeks nor Jews, but of the sect of the Galilæans, why they have preferred their own doctrine to ours; and still farther, why not adhering to the tenets of the Jews, but departing from them, they have taken a peculiar road, assenting to nothing beautiful, no thing worthy, neither among us the Greeks, nor among the Hebrews derived from Moses, but collecting from both nations what is pernicious; impiety, indeed, from the Judaic craft; but a depraved and dissolute life from our indolence and confusion,[*] they think proper to denominate this the most excellent worship of divinity.

The Greeks, therefore, have devised incredible and prodigious fables of the gods. For they say that Saturn devoured his children, and again sent them into the light. They have also feigned illegal marriages. For Jupiter having connexion with his mother, and having begotten children from her, married his own daughter, and in short, after having connexion with her, delivered her up to another. Afterwards follow the lacerations of Bacchus, and the conglutination of his members. And such are the fables of the Greeks.[†]

---

[*] Much indolence and confusion took place in the heathen religion during its decline and fall under the Roman emperors. But this by no means militates against the excellence of that religion; since, as Aristotle justly observes, the best things are subject to the greatest corruptions.

[†] Julian doubtless explained these fables, but Cyril has not given us this explanation. The following explanation, therefore, of them is subjoined, for the sake of the intelligent reader. The meaning of the fable which asserts that Saturn devoured his children and again sent them into the light, is this: Saturn is an intellectual god, or a deity characterised by intellect. But every intellect is converted to itself, seeks itself, and is itself sought. When the fable therefore asserts that Saturn devoured his children, it obscurely signifies this conversion of intellect to itself. But when it says that he again refunded his children into the light, this signifies that intellect not only seeks and procreates, but produces into light and profits.

With respect to the fabulous illegal marriages of the gods, we are informed by Proclus in his MS. Commentary on the Parmenides

Here, however, if you are willing, we will compare the words of Plato with those of Moses. What therefore Plato says of the Demiurgus, and what words he ascribes to him in the fabrication of the world consider, that we may compare the cosmogony of Plato and Moses with each other; for thus it will appear which is the more excellent, and which is more worthy of divinity; whether Plato who worshipped images, or he of whom the Scripture says, that God spoke to him face to face. "In the beginning God created the heavens and the earth.

---

of Plato, that ancient theologists mystically denominated the kindred conjunction and communion of divine causes with each other, marriage. "But this communion," says he, "theologists at one time surveyed in co-ordinate gods, or in divinities possessing the same rank and authority, and then they called it the marriage of Jupiter and Juno, of Heaven and Earth, of Saturn and Rhea. At another time, however, they surveyed this communion in the inferior with the superior gods, and they called it the marriage of Jupiter and Ceres. At another time, on the contrary, they surveyed it in the conjunction of the superior with the inferior divinities, and they called it the marriage of Jupiter and Proserpine." Hence if this communion of gods and goddesses, or in other words, of divine powers of a male with those of a female characteristic, was between divinities of a superior with those of an inferior order, or vice versa, such a conjunction was mystically denominated adultery.

The meaning also of the lacerations of Bacchus, and the conglutination of his members, is as follows: Bacchus is the deity of the mundane intellect, and is fabled to have been torn in pieces by the Titans. But the Titans are the ultimate artificers of things and the most proximate to their fabrications. The laceration, therefore, of the members of Bacchus, signifies the distribution of intellectual life into the universe, by those powers which partially fabricate and proximately preside over mundane natures. Such an intellect, however, remains entire during its participations, and the participations themselves are continually converted to their source, with which they become finally united. So that the illuminations of the mundane intellect, while they proceed into the dark and rebounding receptacle of matter, and invest its obscurity with the supervening ornaments of divine light, return at the same time without intermission to the principle of their descent.

And the earth was without form and void; and darkness was upon the face of the deep. And the spirit of God moved upon the face of the waters. And God said, Let there be light, and there was light. And God saw the light that it was good: and God divided the light from the darkness. And God called the light day, and the darkness he called night. And the evening and the morning were the first day. And God said, let there be a firmament in the midst of the waters, and let it divide the waters from the waters. And God made the firmament, and divided the waters which were under the firmament from the waters which were above the firmament: and it was so. And God called the firmament heaven. And God said, let the waters under the heaven be gathered together unto one place, and let the dry land appear: and it was so. And God said, let the earth bring forth grass, and the fruit tree yielding fruit. And God said, let there be lights in the firmament of the heaven, to divide the day from the night. And God set them in the firmament of heaven, to give light upon the earth; and to rule over the day, and over the night." In this account of the creation, Moses neither says that the abyss was made by God, nor the darkness, nor the water; though it was certainly requisite that he who said of the light that it was produced by the command of God, ought also to have said this of the night, of the abyss, and of the water. Moses, however, says nothing about the fabrication of them, though they are frequently mentioned by him. Besides this, neither does he make mention of the generation or creation of angels, nor of the manner in which they were produced, but alone speaks of the bodies which are contained in the heaven and the earth. So that God, according to Moses, is the fabricator of nothing incorporeal, but is the adorner of the subject matter of the universe. And when he says that the earth was without form and void, these are nothing more than the words of one who makes matter to be a moist and dry essence, and who introduces God as the adorner of it.

Let us, however, compare one with the other, and consider what, and after what manner Divinity fabricates according to Moses, and after what manner he fabricates according to Plato. "And God said, let us make man in our image, after our likeness: and let him have dominion over the fish of the sea, and over the fowl of the air, and over the cattle, and over all the earth, and over every creeping thing that creepeth on the earth. So God created man in his own image, in the image of God created he him; male and female created he them, saying, Be fruitful and multiply, and replenish the earth and subdue it: and have dominion over the fish of the sea, and over the fowl of the air, and over every living thing that moveth upon the earth." Hear now the speech which Plato [in the Timæus] ascribes to the Demiurgus of the universe: "Gods of gods, of whom I am the Demiurgus and father, whatever is generated by me is indissoluble, such being my will in its fabrication. Indeed, every thing which is bound is dissoluble; but to be willing to dissolve that which is beautifully harmonized and well composed is the property of an evil nature. Hence, so far as you are generated, you are not immortal, nor in every respect indissoluble, yet you shall never be dissolved, nor become subject to the fatality of death; my will being a much greater and more excellent bond than the vital connectives with which you are bound at the commencement of your generation. Learn therefore what I now say to you indicating my desire. Three genera of mortals yet remain to be produced.

13

Without the generation of these, therefore, the universe will be imperfect; for it will not contain every kind of animal in its spacious extent. But it ought to contain them, that it may be sufficiently perfect. Yet if these are generated, and participate of life through me, they will become equal to the gods. That mortal natures therefore may subsist, and that the universe may be truly all, convert yourselves according to your nature, to the fabrication of animals, imitating the power which I employed in your generation. And whatever among these is of such a nature as to deserve the same appellation with immortals, which obtains sovereignty in them, and willingly pursues justice, and reverences you,— of this I myself will deliver the seed and beginning: it is your business to accomplish the rest; to weave together the mortal and immortal nature; by this means fabricating and generating animals, causing them to increase by supplying them with aliment, and receiving them back again when dissolved by corruption."

Whether or not this is a dream, learn by under-standing it. Plato denominates gods those apparent natures the sun and moon, the stars, and the heaven. These, however, are the images of unapparent gods; the sun which is visible to the eyes, of the intelligible and unapparent sun; and again, the moon which is apparent to our eyes, and each of the stars are images of intelligibles. Plato, therefore, knew those unapparent gods which are inherent in, co-existent with, and generated and proceeding from the Demiurgus himself. Hence the Demiurgus in Plato very properly says, addressing himself to the unapparent divinities, Gods of gods, viz. of the apparent gods.* But he who fabricated

---

* As this explanation of the epithet "Gods of Gods," given by Julian, is

the heaven, the earth, and the sea, and who generated the stars which are the archetypes of these in intelligibles, is the common Demiurgus of both these. Consider, therefore, that what follows this is well added. Three genera of mortals, says he, yet remain to be produced, viz. men, animals, and plants; for each of these is distinguished by a peculiar nature. If, therefore,

---

not perfectly accurate, and as the whole of this speech of the Demiurgus to the junior gods is unequalled for its sublimity, the following explanation of it is given from the admirable Commentaries of Proclus on the Timæus. "The scope of this speech is to insert demiurgic power and providence in the mundane genera of gods, to lead them forth to the generation of the remaining kinds of animals, and to place them over mortals, analogously to the father of wholes over the one orderly distribution of the universe. For it is necessary that some things should be primarily generated by the demiurgic monad, and others through other media; the Demiurgus, indeed, producing all things from himself, at once and eternally, but the things produced in order, and first proceeding from him, producing together with him the natures posterior to themselves. Thus, for instance, the celestial produce sublunary gods, and these generate mortal animals; the Demiurgus at the same time fabricating these in conjunction with the celestial and sublunary divinities. For in speaking he understands all things, and by understanding all things he also makes the mortal genera of animals; these requiring another proximate generating cause, so far as they are mortal, and through this receiving a progression into being. But the character of the words is enthusiastic, shining with intellectual intuitions, pure and venerable as being perfected by the father of the gods, differing from and transcending human conceptions, delicate and at the same time terrific, full of grace and beauty—at once concise and perfectly accurate. Plato, therefore, particularly studies these things in the imitations of divine speeches; as he also evinces in the Republic, when he represents the Muses speaking sublimely, and the prophet ascending to a lofty seat. He also adorns both these speeches with conciseness and venerableness, employing the accurate powers of colons, directly shadowing forth divine intellections through such a form of words. But in the words before us he omits no transcendency either of the grand and robust in the sentences and the names adapted to these

says he, each of these is generated by me, it will necessarily in every respect become immortal. For nothing else is the cause of immortality to the gods, and the apparent world, than their being generated by the Demiurgus. What then does he say? That whatever is immortal in these, is necessarily imparted by the Demiurgus: but this is the rational soul. Of this,

---

devices, or of magnitude in the conceptions and the figures which give completion to this idea. Besides this, also, much distinction and purity, the unfolding of truth, and the illustrious prerogatives of beauty, are mingled with the idea of magnitude, this being especially adapted to the subject things, to the speaker, and to the hearers. For the objects of this speech are, the perfection of the universe, an assimilation to all-perfect animal [i.e. to its paradigm], and the generation of all mortal animals; the maker of all things, at the same time, presubsisting and adorning all things, through exempt transcendency; but the secondary fabricators adding what was wanting to the formation of the universe. All, therefore, being great and divine, as well the persons as the things, and shining with beauty and a distinction from each other, Plato has employed words adapted to the form of the speech.

"Homer, also, when energizing enthusiastically, represents Jupiter speaking, converting to himself the two-fold co-ordinations of gods; becoming himself, as it were, the centre of all the divine genera in the world, and making all things obedient to his intellection. But at one time he conjoins the multitude of gods with himself without a medium, and at another through Themis as the medium.

> But Jove to Themis gives command to call
> The gods to council.

"This goddess pervading everywhere collects the divine number, and converts it to the demiurgic monad. For the gods are both separate from mundane affairs, and eternally provide for all things, being at the same time exempt from them through the highest transcendency, and extending their providence everywhere. For their unmingled nature is not without providential energy, nor is their providence mingled with matter. Through transcendency of power they are not filled with the subjects of their government, and through beneficent will, they make all things

therefore, I myself will deliver to you, being willing, the seed and beginning: it is your business to accomplish the rest, and to weave together the mortal and immortal nature. It is evident, therefore, that the demiurgic gods receiving from their father a demiurgic power, produced mortal animals on the earth. For if the heaven ought to differ in no respect from man, nor by Jupiter from wild

---

similar to themselves; in permanently abiding, proceeding, and in being separated from all things, being similarly present to all things. Since, therefore, the gods that govern the world, and the dæmons the attendants of these, receive after this manner unmingled purity, and providential administration from their father; at one time he converts them to himself without a medium, and illuminates them with a separate, unmingled, and pure form of life. Whence also I think he orders them to be separated from all things, to remain exempt in Olympus, and neither convert themselves to Greeks nor Barbarians; which is just the same as to say, that they must transcend the two-fold orders of mundane natures, and abide immutably in undefiled intellection. But at another time he converts them to a providential attention to secondary natures, through Themis, and calls upon them to dissect the mundane battle, and excites different gods to different works. These divinities, therefore, especially require the assistance of Themis, who contains in herself the divine laws, according to which providence is intimately connected with wholes. Homer therefore, divinely delivers two-fold speeches, accompanying the two-fold energies of Jupiter; but Plato, through this one speech, comprehends those two-fold modes of discourse. For the Demiurgus renders the gods unmingled with secondary natures, and causes them to provide for, and give existence to, mortals. But he orders them to fabricate in imitation of himself: and in an injunction of this kind, both these are comprehended, viz. the unmingled through the imitation of the father, for he is separate, being exempt from mundane wholes; but providential energy, through the command to fabricate, nourish, and increase mortal natures. Or rather, we may survey both in each; for in imitating the Demiurgus, they provide for secondary natures, as he does for the immortals; and in fabricating they are separate from the things fabricated. For every demiurgic cause is exempt from the things generated by it; but that which is mingled with and filled from them is imbecile and inefficacious, and is unable to adorn

beasts, or serpents, and fishes swimming in the sea; it is necessary that there should be one and the same Demiurgus of all things. But if there is an abundant medium between immortal and mortal natures, which cannot be greater by any addition nor diminished by any ablation with reference to mortal and perishable natures, it is fit that the causes of the one should be

---

and fabricate them. And thus much in common respecting the whole of the speech.

"Let us then, in the first place, consider what we are to under stand by 'Gods of gods,' and what power it possesses: for that this invocation is collective and convertive of multitude to its monad, that it calls upwards the natures which have proceeded to the one fabrication of them, and inserts a boundary and divine measure in them, is clear to those who are not entirely unacquainted with such-like discourses. But how those that are allotted the world by their father are called gods of gods, and according to what conception, cannot easily be indicated to the many; for there is an unfolding of one divine intelligence in these names." Proclus then proceeds to relate the explanations given by others of these words; which having rejected as erroneous, he very properly, in my opinion, adopts the following, which is that of his preceptor, the great Syrianus. "All the mundane gods are not simply gods, but they are wholly gods which participate: for there is in them that which is separate, unapparent, and supermundane, and also that which is the apparent image of them, and has an orderly establishment in the world. And that, indeed, which is unapparent in them is primarily a god, this being undistributed and one: but this vehicle which is suspended from their unapparent essence is secondarily a god, For if, with respect to us, man is two-fold, one inward, according to the soul, the other apparent, which we see, much more must both these be asserted of the mundane gods; since divinity also is two-fold, one unapparent, and the other apparent. This being the case, we must say, that 'Gods of gods' is addressed to all the mundane divinities, in whom there is a connection of unapparent with apparent gods; for they are gods that participate. In short, since two-fold orders are produced by the Demiurgus, some being supermundane, and others mundane, and some being without, and others with participation [of body], if the Demiurgus now addressed the supermundane orders, he would have alone said to them, 'Gods.' for they are without

18

different from the causes of the other.

What occasion, however, have I here to call the Greeks and Hebrews as my witnesses? There is no one who, when praying, does not extend his hands to the heaven; or who, when he swears by god or the gods, possessing in short a conception of a divine nature, does not tend thither. Nor is he improperly affected in this manner. For men perceiving that nothing pertaining to the heavens is either diminished, or increased, or changed, or sustains any passion of disordered natures; but that its motion is harmonic, its order elegant, that the laws of the moon, and the risings and settings of the sun, are definite; and always in definite times, they have very reasonably believed it to be a god, and the throne of god. For a thing of this kind, as being multiplied by no addition, nor diminished by any ablation, and being remote from the mutation according to a change in quality and essence, is free from all corruption and generation.* But being naturally immortal and indestructible, it is pure from every kind of stain. Since, also, it is perpetual and immutable as we see, it is either moved in a circle about the mighty Demiurgus, by a more excellent and divine soul, inhabiting in it, or receiving its motion, from divinity, as our bodies from

---

participation [i.e. without the participation of body], are separate and unapparent:—but since the speech is to the mundane gods, he calls them gods of gods, as being participated by other apparent divinities. In these also dæmons are comprehended; for they also are gods, as to their order with respect to the gods, whose peculiarity they indivisibly participate. Thus also Plato, in the Phædrus, when he calls the twelve gods the leaders of dæmons, at the same time denominates all the attendants of the divinities gods, adding, 'and this is the life of the gods.' All these, therefore, are gods of gods, as possessing the apparent connected with the unapparent, and the mundane with the supermundane."

* This is demonstrated by Aristotle in his Treatise on the Heavens.

the soul which is in us, it evolves an infinite circle, by an unceasing and eternal motion.[*]

Compare with these things the Judaical doctrine, the paradise planted by God, the Adam fashioned by him, and afterwards the woman created for Adam. For God said, it is not good that the man should be alone; I will make an help meet for him. She was not, however, a help meet to him in any thing, but was deceived, and became the cause both to him and herself of being expelled from the delicacies of Paradise. For these things are perfectly fabulous; since how is it reasonable to suppose that God was ignorant that the woman who was made as an help meet for Adam, would rather be pernicious than beneficial to him?

As to the serpent that discoursed with Eve, what kind of language shall we say it used! And in what do things of this kind differ from the fables devised by the Greeks?

Is it not also excessively absurd, that God should forbid men fashioned by himself the knowledge of good and evil? For what can be more foolish than one who is not able to know what is good and what is depraved? For it is evident that such a one will not avoid some things, I mean evils; and that he will not pursue others, viz. such as are good. But, as the summit of all, God forbade man to taste of wisdom: than which nothing is more honourable to man. For that the knowledge of good and evil is the proper work of wisdom, is evident even to the stupid.

Hence the serpent was rather the benefactor, and not the destroyer of the human race. And not this only, but in what Moses afterwards adds, he makes God to be

---

[*] Whatever is produced by an inferior is at the same time produced by a superior cause, and therefore the heavens are both moved by a divine soul inhabiting in them, and by the cause of all.

envious. For after God saw that man participated of wisdom, lest, says he, he should taste of the tree of life, he expelled him from Paradise, clearly saying, "Behold Adam is become as one of us to know good and evil: and now lest he put forth his hand, and take also of the tree of life, and eat, and live forever: Therefore the Lord God sent him forth from the garden of Eden." Each of these narrations, therefore, unless it is a fable containing an arcane theory, which I should think is the case,[*] is full of much blasphemy towards divinity. For to be ignorant that the woman, who was to be the assistant of man, would be the cause of his fall, and to forbid him the knowledge of good and evil, which alone appears to be the connective bond of human life; and besides this to be envious, lest by partaking of life, from being mortal he should become immortal, is the province of a being very envious and malevolent.

But the opinion which they have rightly formed of the God whom they celebrate, that he is the proximate Demiurgus of this world, our fathers have delivered to us from the beginning. For of the natures superior to this God,[†] Moses in short says nothing, as neither has he

---

[*] The Mosaic account of the creation is doubtless a fable derived from the Egyptian mythology, but barbarized by the Jewish narrator.

[†] The immediate artificer of the universe is not the ineffable principle of things: and this not from any defect, but on the contrary, through transcendency of power. For as the essence of the first cause, if it be lawful so to speak, is full of deity, his immediate energy must be deific, and his first progeny must be gods; just as souls are the immediate progeny of one first soul, and natures of one first nature. As the immediate offspring, therefore, of the first cause are wholly absorbed in deity, and are as it were stamped throughout with the characteristics of the ineffable, so as to be *secondarily* what the first god is *primarily*; and as the universe from its *corporeal* subsistence is not a thing of this kind, it is not the *immediate* progeny of the ineffable. Hence, as the world is replete with all various forms, its

ventured to say any thing of the nature of angels; but that they minister to God, he frequently says, and in many places. But whether they are generated, or are unbegotten, or whether they are produced by one cause, and ordered to be ministrant to another, or were produced after some other manner, is nowhere determined. He narrates, however, about the heaven and the earth, and its contents, and after what manner they were adorned. And some things, he says, God ordered to be made, such as the day, and the light, and the firmament; but that he made others, as the heaven and the earth, the sun and the moon. And that some things which had an existence, indeed, but were concealed, he separated, as water and the dry land. Besides this, neither has he ventured to say any thing about the generation, or about the creation of the spirit; but only says, that the spirit of God moved upon the face of the waters. But he does not at all indicate whether it was unbegotten or generated.

Since, therefore, neither about the proximate

---

immediate artificer is a divine essence characterised by intellect, for intellect is the primary seat of forms. At the same time it must be observed, that among causes which produce from their very essence, whatever the inferior cause produces is also produced by the superior; but the manner in which a thing proceeds from the superior transcends that in which it proceeds from the inferior. For processions are according to the characteristics of the natures from which they proceed. Hence, as the first principle of things is ineffable and superessential, all things proceed from him ineffably and superessentially, and other intermediate causes are necessary to the evolution of things into *distinct* subsistence. The Jews, however, as Julian justly observes, appear to have had no conception of any divinity superior to the *immediate* maker of the world, though there are two divine orders prior to that order to which the artificer of the universe belongs, and all these orders are subordinate to the immense principle of things, as is largely shown in the notes to my translation of the Parmenides of Plato.

Demiurgus of this world does Moses appear to have discussed every thing, let us compare with each other the opinion of the Hebrews and of our fathers on this subject. Moses says, that the Demiurgus of the world selected the nation of the Hebrews, paid attention to, and was careful of them alone; but of other nations, he makes no mention whatever, how, or by what gods they are governed, unless some one should grant that he distributed to them the sun and moon. Of these things, however, we shall shortly speak. Thus much, indeed, I will show at present, that Moses himself, and the prophets after him, Jesus of Nazareth also, and *Paul, who surpassed all the magicians and impostors that ever lived,* say, that God is the God of Israel and Judæa alone, and that these are his chosen people. Hear, then, their words, and in the first place those of Moses: "And thou shalt say unto Pharoah, Thus saith the Lord, Israel is my son, even my first born. And I say unto thee, let my son go, that he may serve me; but thou art unwilling to dismiss him." And shortly after: "And they said to him, the God of the Hebrews has called us: let us go, we pray thee, three days' journey into the desert, and sacrifice unto the Lord our God." And again, shortly after, in a similar manner: "The Lord God of the Hebrews hath sent me unto thee, saying, Let my people go, that they may serve me in the wilderness."

But that God paid attention to the Jews alone from the beginning, and that their destiny was illustrious, not Moses only and Jesus, but Paul also appears to have said; though indeed this is not wonderful in Paul. For on every occasion, like the polypus on a rock, he changes the dogmas about divinity; at one time contending that the Jews alone are the inheritance of God: and at another time, persuading the Greeks to join themselves to him, he says, "Is God the God of the Jews only, or also of the heathens? Certainly, he is also the God of the heathens." It is just, therefore, to ask Paul, if God is not the God of the Jews only, but also of the heathens, on what account he sent among the Jews an abundant prophetic spirit, Moses, unction, and the prophets, the law, miracles, and the prodigies of fables; for you hear them exclaiming, "Man eat the bread of angels." And, lastly, why he sent Jesus to them, not a prophet, not unction, not a teacher, not a proclaimer of the philanthropy of God, which would at length be extended to us; but he despised us for myriads, or if you had rather, for thousands of years, leaving all of us in such ignorance as you say, to worship idols,—us, who occupy the earth from the rising to the setting sun, and from the north to the south, except a small race of men, who not more than two thousand years ago inhabited a corner of Palestine. For if he is the God of all of us, and in a similar manner the Demiurgus of all things, why did he despise us? Why, also, is he a jealous God, punishing the sins of the fathers? But all these are partial conceptions, and unworthy of divinity.

Again, therefore, attend to the assertions of our fathers on this subject. For they say, that the Demiurgus is the common father and king of all things, and that to other nations he has distributed gods, who are the prefects of nations, and the curators of cities, each of which governs his own allotment in an appropriate manner. For since in the father all things are perfect, and all things are one, but in the natures distributed from him, a different power has dominion in a different divinity, hence Mars presides over the warlike concerns of nations; Minerva over the same concerns in conjunction with wisdom; but Hermes over such as rather pertain to sagacity than bold undertakings;[*] and thus the nations which are governed by the several divinities follow the essence of their presiding gods. If, therefore, experience does not bear witness to our assertions, let our belief be a fiction, and an unreasonable persuasion: but let yours be praised. But if entirely on the contrary, experience from eternity bears witness to what we say, but nothing anywhere is seen to accord with your assertions, why do you retain this pertinacity? For tell me what is the cause that the Gauls and the Germans are audacious; the Greeks and the Romans, for the most part polished and philanthropic, and at the same time constant and warlike; the Egyptians more sagacious, and excelling in the arts; and the Syrians unwarlike and luxurious, and at the same time of an intelligent, warm, light, and docile disposition? For if no cause of this can be assigned, but they may be rather said to happen from chance, how can it any longer be supposed that the world is governed by Providence? But if any one admits that there are causes of these things, let him by the Demiurgus himself tell me and teach me what they are.

---

[*] Mars is the source of division and motion, separating the contrarieties of the universe, which he also perpetually excites, and immutably preserves, that the world may be perfect and filled with forms of every kind. Hence, also, he presides over war.

Minerva is the summit of all those intellectual natures that reside in Jupiter, the artificer of the world; or, in other words, she is that deity which illuminates all mundane natures with intelligence.

Mercury presides over every species of erudition, leading us to an intelligible essence from this mortal abode, governing the different herds of souls, and dispersing the sleep and oblivion with which they are oppressed. He is, likewise, the supplier of recollection, the end of which is a genuine intellectual apprehension of divine natures. In short, it is the province of this deity to enunciate truth and intellectual light.

For it is very evident, indeed, that human nature has established laws adapted to itself; and that those are political and philanthropic, which very much contribute to nourish the love of mankind; but those savage and inhuman, in which a contrary nature is inherent, and contrary manners. For legislators, through the mode of life which they have instituted, have added but little to the nature and pursuits of mankind; and hence the Scythians received Anacharsis as one agitated with Bacchic fury. Nor in the western nations will you easily find any, except a very few, who are led to philosophize, or geometrize, or who are adapted to any thing of this kind, though the Roman empire is so widely extended. But these nations alone enjoy the gift of speech, and those among them who are very ingenious, are skilled in rhetoric, but they are perfectly ignorant of the mathematical disciplines: So strong does nature appear to be. Whence then arises the difference of manners in nations and legal institutes?

Moses, indeed, assigns a very fabulous cause of the dissimilitude in languages. For he says that the sons of men, assembling together, were willing to build a city, and in it a great tower; but that God said, it was requisite he should descend, and confound their speech. And that no one may think these things are devised by me, we may read what follows in the writings of Moses: "And they said come, let us build us a city and a tower, whose top may reach unto heaven; and let us make us a name, lest we be scattered abroad upon the face of the whole earth. And the Lord came down to see the city and the tower, which the children of men had builded. And the Lord said, Behold the people is one, and they have all one language; and this they begin to do; and now nothing will be restrained from them, which they have imagined to do. Come, let us go down, and there confound their language, that they may not understand one another's speech. So the Lord scattered them abroad from thence upon the face of all the earth: and they left off to build the city and the tower." Do you think fit then to believe in these things, but disbelieve what is related by Homer of the Aloidæ,* who formed the design of placing three mountains on each other, that heaven might be accessible?

> Proud of their strength,
> and more than mortal size,
> The gods they challenge, and affect the skies;
> Heav'd on Olympus tott'ring Ossa stood;
> On Ossa Pelion nods with all his wood.[†]
>
> ODYSS. II. v. 315.

For I say, that the one is in like manner fabulous with the other. But by the gods, why do you who admit the former, reject the fable of Homer? For I think it is proper to be silent among ignorant men about this circumstance, that though all men in every part of the habitable globe should have one voice and one language, yet they would not be able to build a city which would reach to the heavens, though they should convert the whole earth into bricks. For an infinite number of bricks of a magnitude equal to that of the earth, would be requisite to reach as far as the orb of the moon. For let it be supposed that all men assembled together, having one voice and one language, and that the whole earth was

---

* The battle of the giants against the Olympian gods signifies the opposition between the last fabricative powers of the universe and such as are first. And Minerva is said to have vanquished the giants, because she rules over these ultimate artificers of things by her unifying powers.

† The translation is by Pope.

converted into bricks and stones, when would they be able to reach as far as the heavens, though they were drawn out into an extension finer than a thread? Do you, therefore, think that this narration which is so obviously a fable is true? And can you entertain such an opinion of God, as that he was afraid of all mankind having the same language, and that on this account he confounded their speech? And farther still, do you dare to assert this, and pretend that you have at the same time a knowledge of God?

But I return to the same subject. For Moses has informed us how God confounded the speech of men; and he assigns as a cause, that God was afraid lest they should attempt any thing against him, and render heaven accessible to themselves, by having the same language, and being equally wise. But how does he accomplish the affair? By descending from heaven, not being able it seems to effect his purpose without descending on the earth. Neither Moses, however, nor any other, has unfolded the cause of the difference in the manners and legal institutions of men; though, in short, there is a greater difference in the laws and manners of men, than there is in their speech. For what Greek will say that it is necessary to have connexion with a sister, or a daughter, or a mother. This, however, is judged to be good by the Persians. But why is it requisite I should narrate every particular; the love of liberty, and intractable disposition of the Germans; the tractable and mild nature of the Syrians, Persians, and Parthians; and in short of all the barbarians towards the east and the west, and who are delighted to live under more despotic governments. If these things, therefore, take place, without a greater and more divine providence, why should we laboriously investigate things of a greater and more honourable nature, and in vain worship him who providentially attends to nothing? For is it any longer fit that he should require homage from us, who neither pays attention to our life, nor our manners, nor customs, nor equitable legislation, nor political establishment. By no means. See to what a great absurdity such an opinion leads. For of the goods which are surveyed about human life, those of the soul take the lead and those of the body follow. If, therefore, divinity despises the goods pertaining to the souls of us heathens, and neither provides for our natural composition, nor sends us teachers or legislators as he did to the Hebrews, according to Moses and the prophets after him, what is there for which we can be properly grateful to him?

See, however, whether divinity has not given to us those of whom you are ignorant, gods and good prefects, not at all inferior to him who was worshipped from the beginning by the Hebrews, as the presiding deity of Judæa, of which alone he was allotted the guardian care, as Moses says, and those who succeeded him, as far as to you? But if the god worshipped by the Hebrews is the proximate Demiurgus of the world, as we form better conceptions of him than they do, he has also bestowed upon us greater goods than upon them, both pertaining to the soul and externals, of which we shall shortly speak. He has also sent us legislators, in no respect inferior to Moses, but many far superior to him.

What then shall we say, but that unless a certain ethnarchic god presides over every nation, and that under this god there is an angel, a dæmon, and a peculiar genus of souls, subservient and ministrant to more excellent natures, from whence arises the difference in laws and manners,—unless this is admitted, let it be shown by any other how this difference is produced. For it is not sufficient to say, "God said, and it was done"; but it is requisite that the natures of things which are produced should accord with the mandates of divinity. But I will explain more clearly what I mean. God, for instance, commanded that fire should tend upward, and earth downward; is it not, therefore, requisite, in order that the mandate of God may be accomplished, that the former should be light, and the other heavy? Thus, also, in a similar manner in other things. Thus, too, in divine concerns. But the reason of this is, because the human race is frail and corruptible. Hence, also, the works of man are corruptible and mutable, and subject to all-various revolutions. But God being eternal, it is also fit that his mandates should be eternal. And being such, they are either the natures of things, or conformable to the natures of things. For how can nature contend with the mandate of divinity? How can it fall off from this concord? If therefore, as he ordered that there should be confusion of tongues, and that they should not accord with each other, so likewise he ordered that the political concerns of nations should be discordant; he has not only effected this by his mandate, but has rendered us naturally adapted to this dissonance. For to effect this, it would be requisite, in the first place, that there should be different natures of those whose political concerns among nations are to be different. This, indeed, is seen in bodies, if any one directs his attention to the Germans and Scythians, and considers how much the bodies of these differ from those of the Lybians and Æthiopians. Is this, therefore, a mere mandate, and does the air contribute nothing, nor the relation and position of the region with respect of the celestial bodies?

Moses, however, though he knew the truth of this,

concealed it; nor does he ascribe the confusion of tongues to God alone. For he says, that not only God descended, nor one alone with him, but many, though he does not say who they were. But it is very evident, that he conceived those who descended with God to be similar to him. If, therefore, not the Lord only, but those who were with him contributed to this confusion of tongues, they may justly be considered as the causes of this dissonance.

But to what purpose have I been thus prolix? For if, indeed, the God who is proclaimed by Moses is the proximate Demiurgus of the world, we form better opinions of him, who conceive him to be the common Lord of all things; but admit, also that there are other gods who preside over nations, and who are subordinate to him indeed, but being as it were the embassadors of the king, each in a particular manner pays attention to the object of his charge. Nor do we co-arrange the Demiurgus with the gods that are under him. But if Moses, reverencing a certain partial divinity, ascribes to him the government of the universe, it will be better for the Christians being persuaded by us, to acknowledge the God of the universe, together with not being ignorant of that partial deity, than to worship, instead of the Demiurgus of all things, a divinity who is allotted the government of a very small part of the earth.

The law of Moses is wonderful. "Thou shalt not steal; Thou shalt not bear false witness." But each of the precepts are written in the very same words, according to Moses, in which they were written by God himself, "I am the Lord thy God, who brought thee out of the land of Egypt." An other commandment follows: "Thou shalt have no other gods besides me. Thou shalt not make unto thee any graven image"; and he adds the cause:

"For I, the Lord thy God, am a jealous God, visiting the iniquities of the fathers upon the children. Thou shalt not take the name of the Lord thy God in vain. Remember the Sabbath day. Honour thy father and mother. Thou shalt not commit adultery. Thou shalt not kill. Thou shalt not bear false witness. Thou shalt not covet thy neighbour's goods." What nation is there, by the gods, exclusive of the mandates "Thou shalt not worship other gods," and "Remember the Sabbath," which does not think it requisite to observe the other commandments? Hence punishments are established in all nations for those that transgress them, in some more severe, in others similar to those appointed in the laws of Moses; and there is, also, where they are more philanthropic.

But the commandment, Thou shalt not worship other gods, is calumniating divinity in a very high degree. For God is said to be a jealous God; and in another place, to be a consuming fire. When a man, therefore is jealous, and envious, does he appear to you to deserve reprehension; and are you to be considered as divinely inspired, if God is said by you to be jealous? Though how is it reasonable to assert of God a thing which is so manifestly a lie? For if he is jealous, all the gods are adored, he being unwilling, and all other nations worship the gods. Why, therefore, does not he who is so jealous, and who is unwilling that the other gods should be adored, but desirous that himself alone should be worshipped,—why does not he prevent this from taking place? Is he not able; or from the first was he unwilling to forbid the other gods from being worshipped? But the first is impious, to assert that he is not able; and the second accords with our deeds. Abandon, then, this nugacity, and do not draw such great blasphemy upon yourselves.

For if God wished that no one should be adored but himself, why do you adore this son, whom God never thought, nor ever will think to be his own? And this I can easily show. But you, I know not whence, ascribe to him a spurious son.

Why, therefore, is it nowhere seen that God is angry, or indignant with, or swears on account of these things, or rapidly inclines to both sides, as Moses says of Phineas? If any one of you reads the book of Numbers, he will know what I say. For after he who was initiated by Beelphegor, and who had slain with his own hand the woman by whom he had been inveighled, with a shameful and most deplorable wound in the belly, God is made to say, (Numbers xxv. 11.) "Phinehas, the son of Eleazar, the son of Aaron the priest, hath turned my wrath away from the children of Israel, while he was zealous for my sake among them, that I consumed not the children of Israel in my jealousy." What can be more trifling than the cause for which God is falsely made to be angry by the writer of these things? What can be more absurd? If ten or fifteen, or a hundred persons, for they will not say a thousand, but we will suppose that number, had dared to transgress any one of the laws ordained by God, would it be proper that six hundred thousand should be destroyed on account of one hundred thousand? How much better does it appear to me to save one depraved man, together with a thousand most excellent men, than that a thousand worthy men should be destroyed on account of one man? Nor is it fit that the maker of heaven and earth should be so fiercely enraged as frequently to be willing to destroy the race of the Jews. For if the anger of one of the heroes, and of an obscure daemon is difficult to be borne by particular regions and entire cities, who can stand against so great a God, when angry with dæmons, or angels, or men?

It is fit, indeed, to compare this god of Moses with the lenity of Lycurgus, and the clemency of Solon, or with the equity and benignity of the Romans towards malefactors.

Consider, also, from what follows, how much better our affairs are than theirs. Philosophers order us to imitate the gods as much as possible, and say that this imitation consists in the contemplation of real beings.[*]

_____

[*] Thus also Porphyry, in the first book of his admirable treatise "On Abstinence from Animal Food." "The end with us," (i.e. with genuine philosophers) says he, "is to follow the contemplation of true being, promoting as much as possible, by an acquisition of this kind, an inlimitate union of the contemplating individual with the object of contemplation. For in nothing else besides *true being* is it possible for the soul to return to its pristine felicity; nor can this be effected by any other conjunction. But intellect is *true being itself*: so that the proper end is to live according to intellect. For in this material abode, we are similar to those who enter or depart from a foreign region not only in casting aside our native manners and customs, but from the long use of a strange country, we are imbued with affections, manners, and laws, foreign from our natural and true region, and with a strong propensity to these unnatural habits. Such a one, therefore, should not only think earnestly of the way, however long and laborious, by which he may return to his own, but that he may meet with a more favourable reception from his proper kindred, should also meditate by what means he may divest himself of everything alien from his true country, which he has contracted; and in what manner he may best recall to his memory those habits and dispositions, without which he cannot be admitted by his own, and which, from long disuse, have departed from his soul. In like manner it is requisite, if we wish to return to such things as are truly our own, and proper to man considered as a rational soul, to lay aside whatever we have associated to ourselves from a mortal nature, together with all that propensity to material connections, by which the soul is allured, and descends into the obscure regions of sense. But we should be mindful of that blessed and eternal essence intellect, our true father, and hastening our return to the contemplation of the uncoloured light of the good, to take especial

34

Indeed, that this is without passion, and consists in contemplation, is evident, though I should not assert it; because so far as becoming impassive, we apply ourselves to the contemplation of true being, so far we become assimilated to divinity. But what is the imitation of God with the Hebrews? Anger and rage, and savage zeal. "For Phinehas, says God has turned my wrath away, while he was zealous for my sake among the children of Israel." For God finding one who joined with him in being indignant and afflicted, appears to have laid aside his anger. These, and other things of this kind, Moses is made to say of God, in not a few places of the scripture.

That God, however, has not alone paid attention to the Hebrews, but taking care of all nations, has given the Jews, indeed, nothing important or great, but has bestowed upon us things a little more excellent and illustrious, consider from what follows: The Egyptians can enumerate the names of not a few wise men that flourished among them, many of whom were the successors of Hermes, of that Hermes I say, who was the third that came to Egypt. The Chaldæans and Assyrians can enumerate those who descended from Annus and Belus. And the Greeks, an infinite number of those who descended from Chiron. For from him all those who by nature are initiators into mysteries and theologies derived their origin; though the Hebrews appear to consider these two things as alone confined to them.

---

care of these two things; one, that we divest ourselves, as of foreign garments, of every thing mortal and material; the other, how we may return with safety, since thus, ascending to our native land, we are different from ourselves before we descended into mortality. We must, therefore, divest ourselves of the various garments of mortality, by which our vigour is impeded, and enter the place of contest naked, striving for the most glorious of all prizes, the Olympiad of the soul.

[Afterwards, says Cyril, he derides the blessed David and Sampson, and says, that they were not the most strenuous in battle, but far inferior in valour to the Egyptians and Greeks, and scarcely extended their empire to the boundaries of Judæa.]

But God gave science, or the discipline of philosophers, to originate with us. For the theory about the phænomena was perfected by the Greeks, the first astronomical observations being made by the Barbarians in Babylon. But the science of geometry, receiving its beginning from the measurement of the earth in Egypt, has arrived at its present magnitude. The theory of numbers, originating from Phoenician merchants, has at length acquired such a scientific dignity among the Greeks, But the Greeks conjoining these three sciences together with music into one, combining astronomy with geometry, adapting numbers to both, and producing in these an harmonic elegance; hence formed their music, discovering the boundaries of harmonic ratios, and producing an irreprehensible consent, or in the highest degree approaching to it, with the auditory sense.

Whether, therefore, is it requisite that I should severally name the studies, or the men? Such as Plato, Socrates, Aristides, Cimon, Thales, Lycurgus, Agesilaus, Archidamus; or rather the race of philosophers, generals, artificers, legislators. For the most depraved and execrable generals will be found to have used the greatest offenders more equitably than Moses did those who had committed no offence.

What kingdom, therefore, shall I relate to you? Shall I speak of that of Perseus, or of Æacus, or of Minos the Cretan, who having purified the sea from pirates, and having expelled and put to flight the Barbarians, as far as to Syria and Sicily, and thus extended the bounds of his empire, obtained dominion not only over islands, but also over the maritime coast. Dividing, likewise, with his brother Radamanthus, not the lands he had conquered, but his attention to the welfare of mankind. And he, indeed, established laws which he received from Jupiter, who ordered Rhadamanthus to exercise the judicial province.[*]

But *Jesus, who made converts of the worst part of you,* has been celebrated by you for little more than three hundred years: and performed during the whole time that he lived no deed which deserves to be mentioned, unless any one fancies that to cure the blind and the lame, and to exorcise those possessed by dæmons, in the villages of Bethsaida, and Bethania, rank among the greatest undertakings.

[Julian, after this, having spoken largely (says Cyril) of what is related about Dardanus, immediately passes on to the flight of Æneas, and clearly relates the settlement of the Trojans in Italy. He also makes mention of Remus and Romulus, and the manner in which Rome was inhabited; and having said much on this subject, he observes, that the most wise Numa was given to the Romans by Jupiter. He also says of him as follows:]

But after the city was established, it was infested on all sides with many wars. It strenuously, however, opposed and subdued all of them, and becoming increased by these calamitous circumstances, stood in need of greater security. Again, therefore, Jupiter gave it for its governor the most philosophic Numa. This Numa

---

[*] Minos and Rhadamanthus were intellectual heroes illuminated by Jupiter, who raised themselves from the whole of a visible nature to true being, and meddled with mortal concerns no farther than absolute necessity required.

was a most worthy man, passing his time in solitary groves, and in consequence of the purity of his intellectual conceptions, always associating with the gods. He also established most of the laws pertaining to sacred rites.

These things, therefore, as the progeny of divine possessions and inspiration, both from that of the Sybill, and others whom in the language of our country we call prophets, Jupiter appears to have given to the city. And as to the shield which fell from the air,[*] and the head which was found in the hill, whence I think the seat of the mighty Jupiter derived its name,[†] whether shall we number these among the first, or the second of gifts. But you, O unfortunate men! neglecting to adore and reverence the heaven-descended shield which is preserved by us, and which was sent by the great Jupiter, or by the father Mars, as a most certain pledge that he will perpetually defend our city, you adore the wood of a

---

[*] In the reign of Numa, Rome was afflicted with so great a plague, that all seized with it died without any possibility of cure. One day as Numa was going in one of the streets of the city, there fell down from heaven upon him a *holy buckler* or *ancyle*, which he considered as a token of the divine protection; for the plague began to decrease, and the nymph Ægeria told him, that the fate and happiness of his city were annexed to it, as heretofore those of Troy were to the *palladium* of Minerva. In order that the enemies of the Romans might not take away this fatal buckler, Numa caused Veturius Mamurius to make eleven others, so exactly like it, that the holy buckler could never be distinguished from the others. He also placed them in the temple of Mars, under the conduct of twelve priests called Salii. Such is the account given of this shield by ancient historians.

[†] By the seat of the mighty Jupiter, Julian means the Capitol, or the Capitoline mount, which was so denominated from the head of a man called *Tolus*, which was found by the workmen when they were digging the foundation of the temple of Jupiter, who on this account was called *Jupiter Capitolinus*.

cross, marking your forehead with the images of it, and engraving it in the vestibules of your dwellings. Whether, therefore, may any one deservedly hate the more intelligent, or pity the more insane among you, who following you have arrived at such perdition, as to neglect the eternal gods, and betake themselves to a dead body of the Jews.

[After this, Julian having said, that divination is the gift of the gods, observes as follows:]

For the inspiration which arrives to men from the gods, is rare, and exists but in a few. Nor is it easy for every man to partake of this, nor at every time. This has ceased among the Hebrews, nor is it preserved to the present time among the Egyptians. Spontaneous oracles, also, are seen to yield to periods of time.[*] This, however,

---

[*] Van Dale, Fontenelle, and other frivolous writers, have endeavoured to prove that the oracles of the ancients were nothing more than the tricks of fraudulent priests; in answer to whom, I trust it will be sufficient to observe, that to suppose mankind should have been the dupes of such impositions for the space of three or four thousand years would exceed the most extravagant fiction in romance. For how is it possible, even if these priests had been a thousand times more cunning and deceitful than they are supposed to have been, that they could have kept such a secret so impenetrable in every city and province where there were any oracles, as never to have given themselves the lie in any particular? Is it possible that there should never have been one man among them of so much worth as to abhor such impostures? That there should never hare been any so inconsiderate as unluckily to discover all the mystery for want of some precautions? That no man should ever have explored the sanctuaries, subterraneous passages, and caverns, where it is pretended they kept their machines? That they should never have had occasion for workmen to repair them? That only they should have had the secret of composing drugs proper to create extraordinary dreams? And, lastly, That they should have perpetually succeeded one another, and conveyed their machines and their juggling tricks to all those that were to follow them in the same employments from age to age, and from generation to

our philanthropic lord and father Jupiter understanding, that we might not be entirely deprived of communion with the gods, has given to us observation through sacred arts, by which we have at hand sufficient assistance.

I had almost, however, forgotten the greatest of the gifts of the sun and Jupiter: but I have very properly

---

generation, and yet no man have been ever able to detect the imposition?

Besides, who were these priests, that, as it is pretended, were monsters of cruelty, fraud, and malice? They were the most honourable men among the heathens, and such as were most esteemed for their piety and probity. They were, sometimes, magistrates and philosophers. The pontiffs, indeed, and other priests among the Greeks, as well as among the Romans, held the first rank of honour. They were usually taken from noble or patrician families. Plutarch asserts that in some parts of Greece their dignity was equal to that of kings. In the first ages, indeed, kings themselves were often priests, divines, and augurs. This we may learn from Aristotle, in the third book of his Politics, c. 10.; from Cicero de Divin. lib. 1. and de Leg. 1. 2. where he speaks of Romulus and Numa; from Homer, Iliad vi. 1. 73. and Virgil, Æn. 1. 3. when they speak of Helenus, and from the latter, also, when he speaks of king Anius, Æn. iii. 1. 80.

Rex Anius, rex idem hominum, Phœbique sacerdos.

Who can believe that kings, princes, and persons of the first quality were capable of carrying on the trade of jugglers, and amusing the people by delusions and tricks of legerdemain? Plutarch, also, informs us in one of his treatises, that he was himself, to a very old age, the priest of Apollo of Delphi, and that he presided in this character over the oracle, the sacrifices, and all the other ceremonies of this deity, for many years. Depraved as the age is, will any one be hardy enough to assert that a man of such probity, of such gravity of manners, of so much penetration, learning, and judgment as Plutarch, was a cheat and impostor by profession? That he was capable of speaking through a hollow image, to counterfeit the voice of Apollo? Or of suborning a female to act the part of one possessed, when she was seated on the Tripos? There is not surely any one so lost to shame, so devoid of common sense, as to make

preserved it to the last. For it is not peculiar to us only, but is common also, I think, to our kindred the Greeks. For Jupiter, in intelligibles, generated from himself Esculapius; but he was unfolded into light on the earth, through the prolific life of the sun. [Esculapius was a hero of the order of Apollo, who descended from that deity for the benefit of mankind. - TAYLOR] He, therefore,

---

such an assertion.

Very justly, therefore, does Celsus in one of the fragments of his Treatise against the Christians, preserved by Origen, observe as follows respecting these oracles:

"But why is it requisite to enumerate how many things have been foretold, with a divinely inspired voice from oracles, partly by prophetesses and prophetides, and partly by other men and women, under the influence of inspiration? What wonderful things they have heard from the adyta themselves? How many things have been rendered manifest from victims and sacrifices to those who have used them? How many from other prodigious symbols? And to some persons divine appearances have been manifestly present. Of these things, indeed, the life of every one is full. How many cities, likewise, have been raised from oracles, and liberated from disease and pestilence? And how many, neglecting these or forgetting them, have miserably perished? How many colonies have been founded from these, and by observing their mandates have been rendered happy? How many potentates and private persons have, from attending to, or neglecting these, obtained a better or a worse condition? How many, lamenting their want of children, have through these obtained the object of their wishes? How many have escaped the anger of dæmons? How many mutilated bodies have been healed? And again, how many have immediately suffered for insolent behaviour in sacred concerns; some, indeed, becoming insane on the very spot; others proclaiming their impious deeds, but others not proclaiming them [before they perished]; some destroying themselves; and others becoming a prey to incurable diseases? And sometimes a dreadful voice issuing from the adyta themselves has destroyed them."

CELSUS, apud Orig. p. 407.

Again, how could those clear and precise oracles have been produced by fraud, in which what was done in one place was

proceeding from heaven to the earth, appeared uniformly in a human shape about Epidaurus. But thence becoming multiplied in his progressions, he extended his saving right hand to all the earth. He came to Pergamus, to Ionia, to Tarentum, and afterwards to Rome. Thence he went to the island Co, after wards to Ægas; and at length to wherever there is land and sea. Nor did we

_____

foretold in another, as in that famous oracle which was delivered to the ambassadors of Crœsus, and is first mentioned by Herodotus? This fact is as certain as any in antiquity, and is not the only one of this nature. Cicero, Valerius Maximus, Dionysius Halicarnasseus, Strabo, Florus, &c. relate several instances of predictions having been verified in one place of what was doing in another.

It is very justly, indeed, observed by Plutarch, in his treatise concerning the Pythian oracles, that with respect to cursory predictions, some one might foretell that a certain person should be victorious in battle, and he accordingly conquered; that such a city should be subverted, and it was accordingly destroyed; but, says he, *when not only the event is foretold, but how, and when, after what, and by whom it shall be effected, this is no conjecture of things which may perhaps take place, but a premanifestation of things which will absolutely happen.*

Should it be asked why such inspiration, if it once existed, no longer exists at present, it must be observed that the universe being a perfect whole, must have a first, a middle, and a last part. But its first part as having the most excellent subsistence, must always exist according to nature; and its last part must sometimes subsist according to and sometimes contrary to nature. Hence the celestial bodies, which are the first parts of the universe, perpetually subsist according to nature, both the whole spheres, and the multitude co-ordinate to these wholes; and the only alteration which they experience is a mutation of figure, and variation of light at different periods; but in the sublunary region, while the spheres of the elements remain, on account of their subsistence as wholes, always according to nature, the parts of these wholes have sometimes a natural and sometimes an unnatural subsistence; for thus alone can the circle of generation unfold all the variety which it contains.

The different periods in which these mutations happen are very properly called by Plato, in the eighth book of his Republic, periods of *fertility* and *sterility*; for in these periods a fertility or sterility of men, irrational animals, and plants, takes place; so that in fertile

individually, but collectively experience his beneficence. And at one and the same time, he corrected souls that were wandering in error, and bodies that were infirm.

But what thing of this kind can the Hebrews boast as the gift of God, to whom you have fled from us? If, therefore, you have attended to their assertions, you would not have been entirely unfortunate; but though you would have been worse than when you were with us, yet, at the same time, your endurance would have been light and tolerable. For you would have reverenced one God instead of many, and *not a man as you do now, or rather many unfortunate men.* You would also have used a law hard and rough, and having much of the rustic and barbaric, instead of our equitable and philanthropic laws. And, in other things, you would have been in a worse condition, but you would have been more holy and pure with respect to sacred institutions. Now, however, the same thing happens to you as to swallows; for you draw the worst blood from thence, and leave the

---

periods mankind will be both more numerous, and, upon the whole, superior in mental and bodily endowments, to the men of a barren period. And a similar reasoning must be extended to animals and plants. Hence, in fertile periods, when the parts of the earth subsist according to nature, and this is accompanied with a concurrence of proper *instruments*, *times*, and *places*, then divine illumination is abundantly and properly received. But when parts of the earth subsist contrary to nature, as at present, and which has been the case ever since the decline and fall of the Roman empire, then, as there is no longer an aptitude of *places*, *instruments*, and *times*, divine influence can no longer be received, though the illuminations of divine natures continue immutably the same; just, says Proclus, as if a face standing in the same position, a mirror should at one time receive a clear image of it, and at another, one obscure and debile, or, indeed, no image at all. For, as the same incomparable man farther observes, it is no more proper to refer the defect of divine inspiration to the gods, than to accuse the sun as the cause of the moon being eclipsed, instead of the conical shadow of the earth into which the moon falls.

most pure.

For you do not take notice whether any mention is made by the Jews of holiness, but you emulate their rage and their bitterness, overturning temples and altars, and cutting the throats not only of those who remain firm in paternal institutes, but also of those heretics, who are equally erroneous with yourselves, and who do not lament a dead body in the same manner as you do.* For neither Jesus nor Paul exhorted you to act in this manner. But the reason is, that neither did they expect that you would ever arrive at the power which you have obtained. For they were satisfied, if they could deceive maidservants and slaves, and through these married women, and men, such as Cornelius and Sergius; among whom if you can mention one that was at that time an illustrious character, (and these things were transacted under the reign of Tiberius or Claudius,) believe that I am a liar in all things.

This, however, I know not how, has been said by me, as if under the influence of divine inspiration. But that I may return whence I digressed; why, being ungrateful to our gods, have you fled to the Jews? Is it because the gods have given empire to Rome, but to the Jews liberty for a very little time, and perpetual slavery and exile? Consider Abraham, was he not a stranger in a foreign land? Jacob, was he not at first among the Syrians, afterwards in Palestine, and when an old man, a slave among the Egyptians? Did not Moses bring them from the house of bondage, from Egypt, with an elevated arm? And when they inhabited Palestine, did they not change their fortune more frequently than those who have seen the chamæleon say, it changes its colour, at one time

---

* Julian here alludes to the contests between the Arians and Trinitarians.

being obedient to judges, and at another being slaves to those of a different tribe? And when they were under the dominion of kings, (I omit at present how this happened, for neither did God willingly grant that they should be governed by kings, as the scripture says, but this was the effect of compulsion, and when he had previously told them that they would be vilely governed), yet they only inhabited and cultivated their own land a little more than four hundred years. After that time, they were first in subjection to the Assyrians, then to the Medes, then to the Persians, and last of all now to us.

Jesus himself, who is so much celebrated by you, was one of those who were in subjection to Cæsar. If you disbelieve this, I will shortly after demonstrate it to you; or rather let it now be shown. For you say that he was registered together with his father and mother under Cæsar. But after he was born, of what good was he the cause to his kindred? For it is said, they were unwilling to obey him. How, indeed, did that hard-hearted and stony-necked people obey Moses? But Jesus who commanded spirits, who walked on the sea, and expelled dæmons, and, as you say, made the heaven and the earth, (for no one of his disciples dared to say this of him, except John alone, nor he clearly and explicitly), could not change the deliberate choice of his friends and kindred to their own salvation.

Of these things, however, we shall shortly speak when we begin to explore the monstrous deeds and fraudulent machinations of the evangelists. But now answer me this question: Whether is it better to be perpetually free, and for two thousand entire years to have dominion over the greater part of the earth and sea, or to be in subjection, and live in obedience to the mandate of another? There is no one so shameless as to prefer the latter to the former. But who will fancy that it is worse to vanquish in battle, than to be vanquished? Is there any one so insensate? If these things, then, are true, show me one leader of an army among the Hebrews to be compared with Alexander or Cæsar. You have not one to show. Though, by the gods, I well know that I injure these men by the comparison. But I mention these as being known. For there are leaders inferior to these, who are unknown to many, each of which is more admirable than all taken collectively that ever were among the Hebrews.

But the laws of a polity, the form of tribunals, the economy and beauty pertaining to cities, the increase of disciplines, and the exercise of the liberal arts, were only to be seen among the Hebrews in a miserable and barbaric state; though the *depraved Eusebius* pretends that they had hexameter verses among them, and is ambitious to prove that the Hebrews were acquainted with logic, *the name of which he had heard from the Greeks.* What form of medicine ever appeared among the Hebrews, such as that of Hippocrates among the Greeks, and of certain other sects posterior to him?

Is the most wise Solomon to be compared with the Phocylides, or Theognis, or Isocrates of the Greeks? If, indeed, you compare the exhortations of Isocrates with the proverbs of Solomon, I well know you will find that the son of Theodorus surpasses the most wise king. But he, say they, was exercised in the worship of divinity. What then? Did not this Solomon also worship our gods, being deceived, as they say, by a woman? O magnitude of virtue! O riches of wisdom! He had not vanquished pleasure, and the words of a woman perverted him. If, therefore, he was deceived by a woman, do not call this a wise man. But if you believe that he was a wise man, do not think that he was deceived by a woman, but by his own judgment and intelligence, and that he worshipped other gods, in consequence of being persuaded by the doctrine of God who appeared to him. For envy and jealousy do not arrive even as far as to the most excellent men, so far are they from being present with angels and gods. But you are busily employed about partial powers, which he will not err who denominates diabolical* (δαιμονια). For among these powers there is ambition and vain glory; but in the gods there is nothing of this kind.

Why do you apply yourselves to the disciplines of the Greeks, if the reading your writings is sufficient for you? Though it is better to forbid men the reading of them,

---

* This was also the opinion of Porphyry, as is evident from the following most interesting passage, preserved by Augustin in his Treatise De Civit. Lib. XIX. Cap. 23.

"There are terrene spirits of the lowest order, who in a certain terrene place are subject to the power of evil dæmons. From these were the wise men of the Hebrews, of whom Jesus also was one, as you have heard the divine oracles of Apollo above-mentioned assert. From these worst of dæmons, therefore, and lesser spirits of the Hebrew, the oracles forbid the religious, and prohibit from paying attention to them; but exhort them rather to venerate the celestial gods and still more the father of the gods. And we have above shown how the gods admonish us to look to divinity, and everywhere command us to worship him. But the unlearned and impious natures, to whom fate has not granted truly to obtain gifts from the gods, and to have a knowledge of the immortal Jupiter,—these not attending to the gods and divine men, reject, indeed, all the gods, and are so far from hating prohibited dæmons, that they even choose to reverence them. But pretending that they worship God, they do not perform those things through which alone God is adored. For God, indeed, as being the father of all things, is not in want of any thing; but it is well with us when we adore him through justice and continence, and the other virtues, making our life a prayer to him through the imitation and investigation of him. For investigation purifies, but imitation deifies the affection by energizing about divinity."

than the eating consecrated animals. For he who eats of these, as Paul says, is not at all injured; but the conscience of a brother who sees it may, according to you, be scandalized. O wisest of men! . . .* But from these disciplines, whoever among you is naturally of a generous disposition will depart from impiety; *so that even he who has but a small portion of a naturally good disposition, will through these most rapidly abandon your impiety.* It is better, therefore, to restrain men from these disciplines, than from sacred victims. But, as it appears to me, you well know the difference with respect to the acquisition of wisdom between our disciplines and yours. *For from yours no man will become generous and worthy; but from ours every man will become better than himself, though he should be naturally in every respect unapt. But if he possesses an excellent nature, and has received erudition from these, he will then in reality become the gift of God to men, either by enkindling the light of science, or establishing the best form of government, or putting to flight many enemies, and passing through many lands, and a great extent of sea, and through this evincing himself to be an heroic character.* Of the truth of what I assert, this is a clear indication. *Let boys selected from all of you apply themselves to the study of the scriptures, and when they arrive at manhood, if they are at all better than* SLAVES, *consider me as a trifler and insane.* And yet you are so unfortunate and stupid, as to think those writings divine, from which no one will become more wise, or brave, or better than himself. But *those writings from which fortitude, prudence, and justice may be derived, you ascribe to Satan, and those who worship Satan!*

Esculapius heals our bodies; and the Muses, together with Esculapius, Apollo, and the eloquent Hermes, instruct our souls. But Mars and Bellona are our

---

* There is an unfortunate chasm in the original.

associates in battle. Vulcan allots and distributes to us the arts; and all these the motherless virgin Minerva administers in conjunction with Jupiter. Consider, therefore, whether in each of these we are not better than you; I mean in things pertaining to the arts, wisdom, and intelligence? Whether you consider those arts which pertain to the indigence of human life, or those imitative arts which are for the sake of the beautiful, such as statuary, painting, and medicine the gift of Esculapius, whose oracles are in every part of the earth, and of which the gods give us continually to partake. Hence, Esculapius has frequently restored me to health by indicating remedies. And of these things Jupiter is a witness. If, therefore, we, who have given ourselves up to the spirit of apostacy, are better than you in things pertaining to the soul, to the body, and to externals; why abandoning these, do you betake your-selves to those?

Why, also, do you neither continue in the doctrine of the Hebrews, nor embrace the law which God gave them; but abandoning paternal rites, and giving yourselves up to those whom the prophets proclaimed, dissent more from them than from us? For if any one wishes to consider the truth respecting you, he will find that your impiety is composed from the Judaic audacity, and the indolence and confusion of the heathens. For deriving from both not that which is most beautiful, but the worst, you have fabricated a web of evils. With the Hebrews, indeed, there are accurate and venerable laws pertaining to religion, and innumerable precepts which require a most holy life and previous choice. But when the Jewish legislator forbids the serving all the gods, and enjoins the worship of one alone, whose portion is Jacob, and Israel the line of his inheritance, and not only says this, but also adds, I think, you shall not revile the gods, the detestable wickedness and audacity of those in after-times, wishing to take away all religious reverence from the multitude, thought that not to worship should be followed by blaspheming the gods. This you have alone thence derived; but there is no similitude in any thing else between you and them. Hence, from the innovation of the Hebrews, you have seized blasphemy towards the venerable gods; but from our religion you have cast aside reverence to every nature more excellent than man, and the love of paternal institutes; and have alone retained the eating of all things, in the same manner as herbs. And if it be requisite to speak the truth, you have ambitiously endeavoured to extend your confusion. This, however, I think happens very properly, that you have conceived your doctrines ought to be adapted to all nations and lives of other men, such as *inn-keepers, publicans, dancers, and others of the like kind!*

That not only, however, the Christians of the present age, but also those who from the beginning received the word from Paul, were such men as these, is very evident from what Paul testifies, when writing to them. For I do not think he was so impudent as to have said of them so many disgraceful things in his letter, if he had not known them to be true. Of these, however, if he wrote so many things in their praise, and they were true, he ought to have blushed; but if they were false and fictitious, he ought by concealing them to have avoided appearing to employ effeminate blandishments and illiberal flattery. What Paul, however, writes to them about his auditors is as follows: "Be not deceived, neither *fornicators*, nor *idolaters*, nor *adulterers*, nor *effeminate*, nor *abusers of themselvers with mankind*, nor *thieves*, nor *covetous*, nor *drunkards*, nor *revilers*, nor *extortioners*, shall inherit the kingdom of God. And of these things, brethren, you are not ignorant, *because you also were such*;* but ye are *washed*, but ye are *sanctified*, but ye are *justified in the name of the Lord Jesus.*"† You see, then, that they were such characters as these, but they were sanctified and washed, water being sufficient to wipe away and purify, which penetrates as far as to the soul! And baptism, indeed, does not take away the spots of leprosy, nor ring-worms, nor warts, nor the gout, nor the dysentery, nor the dropsy, nor the reduvia,‡ nor any small or great defect of the body, but it can take away

---

* There is some difference here between this and the vulgar translation.

† What is here asserted of the Christians by Julian, is also confirmed by Celsus in the following passage preserved by Origen.

"That I do not, however, accuse the Christians more bitterly than truth compels, may be conjectured from hence; that the cryers who call men to other mysteries proclaim as follows; Let him approach whose hands are pure, and whose words are wise. And again, others proclaim: Let him approach who is pure from all wickedness, whose soul is not conscious of any evil, and who leads a just and upright life. And these things are proclaimed by those who promise a purification from error. Let us now hear who those are that are called to the Christian mysteries; *Whoever is a sinner, whoever is unwise, whoever is a fool, and whoever, in short, is miserable, him the kingdom of God will receive.* Do you not, therefore, call a sinner, an unjust man, a thief, a house breaker, a wizard, one who is sacrilegious, and a robber of sepulchres? What other persons would the cryer nominate, who should call robbers together?"

CELSUS, p. 147.

The methodists, who are the genuine Christians, or who at least have the genuine spirit of Christianity, call upon such characters at the present day, and boldly assert that God is better pleased with such sinners than with men who trust for their salvation to integrity of conduct, and a uniform cultivation of the moral virtues; such men, according to their diabolical cant, being odious to God, as trusting to the filthy rags of their own righteousness!

‡ i.e. The looseness of the skin about the roots of the nails of the fingers.

adultery, rapine, and, in short, all the crimes of the soul!!!

Since, however, they say that they differ from the Jews of the present time, but that they are accurately Israelites, according to the prophets of the Jews, and that they especially believe in Moses, and the prophets derived from him in Judæa, let us see in what they particularly accord with them. But let us begin from Moses, who they say predicted the future nativity of Jesus. Moses, therefore, not once, nor twice, nor thrice, but very frequently thinks it fit that one God alone should be honoured, whom he denominates supreme. But he never says that any other god is to be worshipped, though he speaks of angels and lords, and many gods. He considers, however, the first god as transcendent, but does think that there is any other who ranks as second, neither similar nor dissimilar to him, according to your fabrication. But if there is with you one word of Moses in favour of these things, it is just you should produce it. For the words, "The Lord our God will raise up a prophet for you among your brethren, like unto me; unto him ye shall hearken;" (Deut. xviii. 15.) are by no means said of the son of Mary. But if any one should grant for your sake that they were said of Jesus, yet Moses says he will be like him, and not God; a prophet like himself, and originating from men, and not from God. And the words, "The sceptre shall not depart from Judah, nor a lawgiver from between his feet," (Gen. xlix. 10.) are by no means said of Christ, but of the kingdom of David, which appears to have ended in the Sedecian king. And the scripture, indeed, has a two-fold reading; "Until those things shall come that are deposited for him;" but you adulterate these words, "Until he shall come for whom these things are deposited." But that none of these things pertain to Jesus is very evident. For neither is he from Judah; since how is it possible he should who according to you was not born from Joseph, but from the holy spirit? For, genealogizing Joseph, you refer him to Judah; and yet you have not been able to feign this well. For Matthew and Luke may be confuted, being discordant with each other about his genealogy.

The discussion of this, however, we shall omit, as we intend accurately to explore the truth of it, in the second book. Let it then be granted that his sceptre was from Judah, yet he was not God from God, according to what is said by you; nor were all things made by him, and without him no thing was made. But it is also said in Numbers, "A star shall arise from Jacob, and a man from Israel." (Num. xxiv. 17.) That this pertains to David, and his descendants, is very evident. For David was the son of Jesse. If, therefore, you can prove what you assert from these words, demonstrate that you can, deriving one word from thence, whence I have taken many. But that Moses thought his one God to be the God of Israel, he says in Deuteronomy, "That thou mightest know that the Lord thy God is one, and there is none else beside him." (Deut. iv. 35.) And again, " Know therefore this day, and consider it in thine heart, that the Lord thy God is God in heaven above, and upon the earth beneath : there is none else." (Deut. iv. 39). And again, "Hear, O Israel, the Lord our God is one Lord." (Deut. vi. 4.) Again, also, "See that I am, and there is no God besides me." These things, therefore, Moses says, contending that there is only one God. But they, also, perhaps will say, neither do we assert that there are two or three gods. I, however, will show that they do assert this, adducing the testimony of John, who says, "In the beginning was the word, and the word was with God, and the word was

God." You see that he is said to be with God. But whether this is said of him who was born from Mary, or of any other, that at the same time I may answer Photinus, is at present of no consequence, for I leave this contest to you. This, however, is sufficient as a testimony, that John says he was with God, and in the beginning. How, therefore, do these things accord with what Moses says? But they accord, say they, with the words of Isaiah, "Behold a virgin shall conceive and bear a son." (Isaiah vii. 14.) Let it be admitted that this is said of God, though this is by no means the case; for she who was married, was not a virgin; and before she was delivered, she had had connection with her husband; but let this be admitted, does he say that God will be born of a virgin? You, however, do not cease to call Mary the *God-producer*, (*θεοτοκος*) Or, does he say that he who will be born from a virgin is the only-begotten son of God, and the first born of every creature? But can any one show among the words of the prophets, that which is asserted by John, "All things were made by him, and without him was not any thing made?" Hear, however, afterwards what we show from the writings of the prophets: "O Lord our God, keep us; beside thee we know of no other." And King Hezekiah is represented by them praying, "O Lord God of Israel, who sittest between the cherubims, thou art God alone." (Isaiah xxxvii. 16.) Does he, then, leave any place for a second?

If, however, the word is according to you, God from God, and is born from the essence of the father, why do you say that the virgin is the god-producer? For how could she produce a god, being human, such as we are? Besides, when God clearly says, "I am, and there is not any saviour besides me," will you dare to call him the saviour who was born from Mary?

But that Moses denominates angels gods, hear from his own words: "The sons of God saw the daughters of men that they were fair; and they took them wives of all which they chose." And a little after he adds, "And also after that, when the sons of God came in unto the daughters of men, and they bare children to them, the same were giants, which were of old, men of renown." (Gen. vi. 2 and 4.) That he means angels, therefore, by the sons of God, is very evident: and that this is not a forced interpretation, is manifest from his saying, that not men, but giants, were produced from them. For if he had thought that men were their fathers, and not some more excellent and robust nature, he would evidently not have said that giants were their offspring. For he appears to me to signify that the race of giants derived its subsistence from the mixture of the mortal and immortal nature. Would not, then, he who names many sons of God, and these not men, but angels, would not he have unfolded to men the only-begotten word, or son of God, or in whatever manner you may call him, if he had known him? But because he thought this a great thing, he says of Israel, "My first-born son, Israel." (Exod. iv. 22.) Why, therefore, did not Moses say this of Jesus? He taught, indeed, that there is only one God, and that many of his sons are distributed among the nations, but he neither knew from the beginning, nor does he clearly teach any thing about the first born son, or God, the word, or any of those things which afterwards were falsely devised by you. Hear, then, Moses and the other prophets. Moses, indeed, asserts many such things, and everywhere. "Thou shalt fear the Lord thy God, and him only shalt thou serve." (Deut. vi. 13.) How then is Jesus in the gospels said to have commanded, "Go ye, therefore, and teach all nations, baptizing them in the name of the father, and of the son, and of the holy ghost," if they were to adore him also? You, likewise, conceiving in conformity to this, theologize about the son in conjunction with the father.

Hear again, therefore, what Moses says of the Averrunci:* "And he shall take of the congregation of the children of Israel two kids of the goats for a sin offering, and one ram for a burnt offering. And Aaron shall offer his bullock of the sin offering, which is for himself, and make an atonement for himself and his house. And he shall take the two goats, and present them before the Lord, at the door of the tabernacle of the congregation. And Aaron shall cast lots upon the two goats; one lot for the Lord, and the other lot for the scapegoat, and he shall be sent, says he, into the wilderness." (Levit. xvi. 5, 6, &c). The goat, therefore, that is to be sent as a scapegoat, is to be sent in this manner. But "then, says he, shall he kill the goat of the sin offering that is for the people, and bring his blood within the vail, and do with that blood as he did with the blood of the bullock, and sprinkle it upon the mercy seat, and before the mercy seat. And he shall make an atonement for the holy place, because of the uncleanness of the children of Israel, and because of their transgressions in all their sins." (Levit. xvi. 15, 16).

That Moses, therefore, knew the modes of sacrifices is very evident from what has been said. And that he did not conceive them to be impure as you do, again hear from his own words: "But the soul that eateth of the flesh of the sacrifice of peace offerings, that pertain unto

---

*   i.e. *Gods who avert misfortunes and evil accidents.* Apollo and Hercules were of the number of these gods among the Greeks, as Castor and Pollux among the Romans, and they were from hence called ἀποτρόπαιοι, viz. those who averted evil.

the Lord, having his uncleanness upon him, even that soul shall be cut off from his people." (Levit. vii. 20). Moses himself was truly religious about the eating of victims.

But it is proper after this that you should recollect what has been before said, and for the sake of which these things also have been mentioned. For why, since you have revolted from us, do you not embrace the law of the Jews, and abide in what is enjoined by them? Some one who *sees acutely* will perhaps say, Neither did the Jews sacrifice. But I will prove that the sight of such a one is *dreadfully dull*. In the first place, because neither do you preserve any other of the legal rites of the Jews. In the second place, because the Jews sacrifice in their houses, and even now they eat all the victims, pray before they sacrifice, and give the right hand shoulder as first fruits to the priests. Being now, however, deprived of a temple and altar, or as they are accustomed to say, of a sanctuary, they are prevented from offering the first fruits of the victims to God. But you who have discovered a new sacrifice, since you are not in want of Jerusalem, why do you not sacrifice? Though, indeed, I say this to you superfluously, since I said it before, when I wished to show that the Jews accorded with the heathens, except in believing that there is only one God. For that is peculiar to them, but foreign from us. Everything else, indeed, is common to us, temples, sacred groves, altars, lustrations, and certain things to be observed; in which we either do not at all, or but little, differ from each other.

Why, too, are you not similarly pure in diet with the Jews? But you say it is requisite to eat all things as if they were pot-herbs, believing in Peter because he said, "What God hath cleansed, that call not thou common."

(Acts x. 15). Is this to be considered as an argument, that God formerly thought them defiled, and that now he has made them pure? For Moses speaking of quadrupeds says, "Whatsoever parteth the hoof and is cloven-footed, and cheweth the cud, is clean," (Levit. xi. 3.); "but that which is not of this kind is unclean." (Deut. xiv. 7), If. therefore, the hog, from the vision of Peter, now ranks among those animals that chew the cud, shall we believe in him? For it would be truly prodigious if he should have this faculty after the vision of Peter. But if Peter feigned that he saw this *revelation,* that I may speak after your manner, at the tanner's house, why do you so readily assent in a thing of such consequence? For what difficult thing would he have enjoined you, if he had forbidden you to eat, besides swine, winged and aquatic animals, affirming that these also, as well as those, are rejected by God, and considered as impure?

But why am I thus prolix in relating what is said by them, when it may be seen whether their assertions possess any strength? For they say that God besides the former established a second law. That the former law was for a season circumscribed by a definite time; but that this posterior law made its appearance, because it was adumbrated in the time and by the type of Moses. That they assert this, however, falsely, I will clearly demonstrate, producing from Moses not only ten, but a thousand testimonies, in which he says, that the law is eternal. But now hear from Exodus: "And this day shall be unto you for a memorial; and ye shall keep it a feast to the Lord, *throughout your generations;* ye shall keep it a feast by an ordinance forever. Seven days shall ye eat unleavened bread; even the first day shall ye put away leaven out of your houses." (Exod. xii. 24, 25).

[After this Julian, according to Cyril, cites other passages, in which he shows that the law is denominated eternal. He then adds as follows:]

Omitting many passages of this kind on account of their multitude, in which it is said that the law of Moses is eternal, do you show me where that is which Paul after this had the audacity to say, viz. "That Christ is the end of the law?" Where does God promise to the Hebrews another law besides that which was established? Nowhere: nor does he promise a correction of the established law. For again, hear Moses: "Ye shall not add unto the word which I command, neither shall ye diminish ought from it. Keep the commandments of the Lord and his statutes, which I command thee this day for thy good. And cursed is every one who does not abide in all things." (Deut. iv. 10, &c.) But you think it a trifle to take away from and add to what is written in the law. You, also, think that to transgress it entirely is a proof of greater fortitude and magnanimity, not looking to truth, but to that which is calculated to persuade the multitude.

[Cyril, also, informs us that Julian calls Peter a hypocrite, and says that he was reproved by Paul, because at one time he endeavoured to live according to the customs of the Greeks, and at another according to those of the Jews.* Afterwards he adds:]

But you are so unfortunate that neither do you abide in those things which were delivered to you by the apostles; and these by those that succeeded them were rendered worse and more impious. Neither Paul, therefore, nor Matthew, nor Luke, nor Mark dared to say

---

* The becoming all things to all men, was doubtless a part of the creed of Peter as well as of Paul.

that Jesus is God; but *good John,* perceiving that now a great multitude in many of the Grecian and Italian cities were infected with this *disease;* and hearing, as it appears to me, that the sepulchres of Peter and Paul were privately indeed, but at the same time hearing that they were worshipped, was the first that dared to assert this.

[After this, says Cyril, Julian having said a little about John the Baptist, returns to the word which was proclaimed by John the Evangelist.]

And "the word," says he, "was made flesh, and dwelt among us," (John i.); but he was ashamed to say how. He, likewise, never calls him either Jesus or Christ, while he calls him God and the word. But gradually and fraudulently as it were deceiving our ears, he says that John the Baptist gave this testimony of Jesus Christ, viz. that it is requisite to believe him to be God the word.

I will not, however, deny that John says this of Jesus Christ; though it appears to some of the impious among you, that Jesus Christ is one person, and the word proclaimed by John another. But this is not the case. For he whom he says is God the word, is the Christ Jesus that was known by John the Baptist. Consider, therefore, how cautiously, gradually, and privately he introduces the colophon of impiety to the drama; for he is so crafty and fraudulent, that he again retracts what he had said, adding, "No man hath seen God at any time; the only begotten son which is in the bosom of the father, he hath declared him." Whether, therefore, is this God the word who was made flesh, the only-begotten son which is in the bosom of the father? And if, indeed, it is as I think it is, you also have certainly seen God. For he dwelt among you, and you beheld his glory. Why, therefore, do you say that no one has ever seen God? For you have beheld, if not God the father, yet certainly God the word. But if the only-begotten God is one person, and God the word another, as I have heard some of your sect assert, neither John it seems has any longer dared to say this.

This evil, however, received its beginning from John. But who can execrate as it deserves what you have invented in addition to this, by introducing many recent dead bodies to that ancient dead body? You have filled all places with sepulchres and monuments, though it is never said by you anywhere, that you are to roll about sepulchres and worship them. But you have proceeded to that degree of depravity, as to think that not even the words of Jesus of Nazareth are to be attended to on this subject. "Woe unto you scribes and pharisees, hypocrites! for ye are like unto whited sepulchres, which indeed appear beautiful outward, but are within full of dead men's bones, and of all uncleanness." (Matt, xxiii. 27). If, therefore, Jesus says that sepulchres are full of uncleanness, how is it that you invoke God upon them?

[To this Julian adds, that when a certain disciple said to Christ, "Lord suffer me to go and bury my father," he answered him, "Follow me, and let the dead bury the dead." (Matt. viii. 21).]

This, then, being the case, why do you roll about sepulchres? Are you willing to hear the cause? Not I, but the prophet Isaiah will tell it. "They sleep in sepulchres and caves on account of dreams."* (Isaiah lxv. 4.) Consider, therefore, how this work of incantation, to sleep in sepulchres for the sake of dreams, was resorted to by the Jews of old. It is probable that your apostles after the death of their master, doing the very same

---

* The vulgar translation is, "Which remain among the graves, and lodge in the monuments."

thing, delivered it to you who were the first believers from the beginning, and that they performed the incantation more according to the rules of art than you; but to those that came after them publicly exhibited the work-shops of this incantation and execrable employment.

You, however, apply yourselves to those things which God from the beginning execrated, both through Moses and the prophets; but you refuse to bring victims to the altar and to sacrifice. For fire does not descend as in the time of Moses, to consume the victims.* This once took place under Moses, and again under Elias the Thesbite, a long time after. That Moses, however, thought it re quisite that adventitious fire ought to be introduced, and farther still, the patriarch Abraham prior to him, I will briefly show.

[Cyril then observes, that Julian having reminded the reader of the history of Isaac, again adduces Abel as an example, and says, that he when he sacrificed had not fire from heaven, but that it was externally brought to the altars. He also inquires why God praised the sacrifice of Abel, but rejected that of Cain; and what the meaning is of those words, "If you rightly offer, but do not rightly divide, will you not sin? Be quiet." (Gen. iv. &c.) Julian endeavours to adapt these words to the divination pertaining to victims. For, says he, the sacrifice to God through animals is more acceptable to him than the sacrifice from the fruits of the earth.]

And not this only, but also when the sons of Adam offered first fruits to God, Moses says, "And the Lord had respect unto Abel, and to his offering: But unto Cain and

---

* Servius, in his Commentary on Virgil, says, that formerly fires were not kindled on altars, but drawn from heaven by prayer; *apud majores aræ non incendebantur, sed ignem divinum precibus eliciebant.*

his offering, he had not respect. And Cain was very wroth, and his countenance fell. And the Lord said unto Cain, Why art thou wroth? and why is thy countenance fallen? If thou offerest rightly, but dost not divide rightly, dost thou not sin?" (Gen. iv. 4, &c.) Do you desire, therefore, to hear what were their offerings? "And in process of time it came to pass, that Cain brought of the fruit of the ground an offering unto the Lord. And Abel he also brought of the firstlings of his flock, and of the fat thereof," (Gen. iv. 3.) Yes, say they, God does not blame the sacrifice, but the division; for he says to Cain, "If thou offerest rightly, but dost not divide rightly, dost thou not sin?" For this one of their *all-wise bishops* said to me. This bishop, however, deceived himself in the first place, and afterwards others. For being asked after what manner the division was blameable, he had nothing to say, nor could he even give me a frigid explanation of it. Perceiving, therefore, that he was perplexed, I said this very thing which you say, God rightly blamed. For with respect to alacrity, it was equal in both, because both thought it was proper to offer gifts and sacrifices to God. But with respect to the division, the one hit the mark, but the other deviated from it. In what manner, however? Since of things on the earth, some are animated, but others inanimate; and the animated are more honourable than the inanimate with the living God, and the cause of life, so far as they participate of life, and are more allied to soul; on this account God was delighted with him who offered a perfect sacrifice.

That I may, however, repeat to them what I have said: Why are you not circumcised? Paul says "they assert that circumcision is of the heart, and not of the flesh"; and that he believes in the unholy words, proclaimed both by himself and Peter. But hear again, that God is said to have given the circumcision according to the flesh, as a covenant and a sign to Abraham. "This is my covenant which ye shall keep between me and you, and thy seed after thee; every man child among you shall be circumcised. And ye shall circumcise the flesh of your foreskin; and it shall be a token of the covenant between me and you." (Gen. xvii. 10).

[Julian also adds to these things, that Christ himself says that the law ought to be preserved; for his words are: "Think not that I am come to destroy the law or the prophets: I am not come to destroy, but to fulfil." (Matt. v. 17.) And again, "Whosoever, therefore, shall break one of these least commandments, and shall teach men so, he shall be called the least in the kingdom of heaven." (Matt. v. 19.)]

Since, therefore, Christ has indubitably commanded the law to be preserved, and has appointed punishments for those who break even one of those mandates, but you in short break all of them, what mode of apology can you invent? For either Jesus speaks falsely, or you are not perfectly observers of the law.

[Cyril adds, that Julian also accuses the Galilæans, that they neither keep the Sabbath, nor immolate a lamb after the manner of the Jews, nor eat unleavened bread; and that the only pretext which is left them for this negligence, is, that it is not lawful for those to sacrifice who are out of Jerusalem.]

"Circumcision will be about thy flesh," says Moses. (Gen. xvii.) But neglecting this, the Galileans say, that they are circumcised in their hearts. Perfectly so. For no one among you is vicious, no one is depraved; you are so circumcised in your hearts! It is well. We are not able, say they, to observe the precept about unleavened bread and the passover; for Christ was once sacrificed for us, and afterwards he forbids us to eat unleavened bread. By the Gods, indeed, though I am one of those who are averse to celebrate the festivals of the Jews, yet I always adore the God of Abraham, Isaac, and Jacob, who being themselves Chaldæans of a sacred and theurgic race, learnt circumcision from the Egyptians while they dwelt among them. The Jews worship that God, however, who to me, and to those who worship him as Abraham did, was propitious, being a very great and powerful God, but not at all pertaining to you. For you do not imitate Abraham, by raising altars to him, and worshipping him with sacrifices as he did.

For Abraham sacrificed always and continually just as we do; and in consequence of this he used the most excellent divination. This also, perhaps, was Grecian; but he employed augury in a greater degree than the Greeks. He had, likewise, a symbolical guardian of the house. But if any one of you disbelieves this, I will clearly show you what Moses says on the subject. "After these things the word of the Lord came unto Abraham in a vision of the night, saying, Fear not Abraham, I am thy shield and thy exceeding great reward. And Abraham said, Lord God what wilt thou give me, seeing I go childless, and the steward of my house is this Eliezer of Damascus? And behold the word of the Lord came unto him, saying, This shall not be thine heir; but he that shall come forth out of thine own bowels shall be thine heir. And he brought him forth abroad, and said, Look now toward heaven, and tell the stars if thou be able to number them: and he said unto him, so shall thy seed be. And he believed in the Lord; and he counted it to him for righteousness," (Gen. xv. 1, &c.) Here tell me why the angel or God that gave the oracle, brought him forth and shewed him the stars? For did he not know, while he was in the house, what a great multitude there was of stars which are perpetually apparent, and glitter by night? But I think he was willing to shew him the shooting stars, in order that the decree of heaven, which governs and confirms all things, might produce a clear belief in his words.

Lest, however, some one should think that an interpretation of this kind is forced, I will confirm it by adding the words which immediately follow: "And he said unto him, I am the Lord that brought thee out of Ur of the Chaldæans, to give thee this land to inherit it. And he said, Lord God, where by shall I know that I shall inherit it? And he said unto him, Take me an heifer of three years old, and a she-goat of three years old, and a ram of three years old, and a turtle-dove, and a young pigeon. And he took unto him all these, and divided them in the midst, and laid each piece one against another; but the birds divided he not. And when the birds came down upon the carcases, *Abraham sat together with them.*"[*] Take notice, therefore, that, the prediction of the angel or God who appeared, was confirmed by augury, and not as you say carelessly, but the divination was effected in conjunction with sacrifice. But he says, that by the flight of birds he will show that the promise is firm.

[Julian admits, however, the faith of Abraham, adding, that faith without truth is folly and rage; and that truth does not consist in mere words, but it is requisite that some clear sign should also follow the words, which when it happens, gives credibility to the prediction.]

---

[*] The vulgar translation is, "*Abraham drove them away.*"

EXTRACTS

FROM

THE OTHER WORKS

OF

THE EMPEROR JULIAN
RELATIVE TO THE CHRISTIANS

EXRACT

As the founder of your city is Alexander, and your ruler and tutelar deity King Serapis, together with the virgin his associate, and the Queen of all Egypt, Isis, . . . you do not emulate a healthy city, but the diseased part dares to arrogate to itself the name of [the whole] city. By the gods, men of Alexandria, I should be very much ashamed, if, in short, any Alexandrian should acknowledge himself to be a Galilæan.

The ancestors of the Hebrews were formerly slaves to the Egyptians. But now, men of Alexandria, you, the conquerors of Egypt (for Egypt was conquered by your founder), sustain a voluntary servitude to the despisers of your national dogmas, in opposition to your ancient sacred institutions. And you do not recollect your former felicity, when all Egypt had communion with the gods, and we enjoyed an abundance of good. But, tell me, what advantage has accrued to your city from those who now introduce among you a new religion? Your founder was that pious man Alexander of Macedon, who did not, by Jupiter! resemble any one of these, or any of the Hebrews who far excelled them. Even Ptolemy, the son of Lagus, was also superior to them. As to Alexander, if he had encountered, he would have endangered even the Romans. What then did the Ptolemies, who succeeded your founder? Educating your city, like their own daughter, from her in fancy, they did not bring her to maturity by the discourses of Jesus, nor did they construct the form of government through which she is now happy, by the doctrine of the odious Galilæans.

Thirdly, After the Romans became its masters, taking it from the bad government of the Ptolemies, Augustus visited your city, and thus addressed the citizens: "Men of Alexandria, I acquit your city of all blame, out of regard to the great god Serapis, and also for the sake of the people, and the grandeur of the city. A third cause of my kindness to you is my friend Areus." This Areus, the companion of Augustus Cæsar, and a philosopher, was your fellow-citizen.

The particular favours conferred on your city by the Olympic gods were, in short, such as these. Many more, not to be prolix, I omit. But those blessings which the apparent gods bestow in common every day, not on one family, nor on a single city, but on the whole world, why do you not acknowledge? Are you alone insensible of the splendor that flows from the sun? Are you alone ignorant that summer and winter are produced by him, and that all things are alone vivified, and alone germinate from him? Do you not, also, perceive the great advantages that accrue to your city from the moon, from him and by him the fabricator of all things? Yet you dare not worship either of these deities; but this Jesus, whom neither you nor your fathers have seen, you think must necessarily be God the word, while him, whom from eternity every generation of mankind has seen, and sees and venerates, and by venerating lives happily, I mean the mighty sun, a living, animated, intellectual, and beneficent image of the intelligible father, you despise. If, however, you listen to my admonitions, you will by degrees return to truth. You will not wander from the right path, if you will be guided by him, who, to the twentieth year of his age, pursued that road, but has now worshipped the gods for near twelve years.

EXRACTS

FROM

THE FRAGMENT OF AN ORATION OR EPISTLE ON
THE DUTIES OF A PRIEST.

IF any are detected behaving disorderly to their prince, they are immediately punished; but those who refuse to approach the gods, are possessed by a tribe of evil dæmons, who driving many of the atheists [i.e. of the Christians] to distraction, make them think death desirable, that they may fly up into heaven, after having forcibly dislodged their souls. Some of them prefer deserts to towns; but man, being by nature a gentle and social animal, they also are abandoned to evil dæmons who urge them to this misanthropy; and many of them* have had recourse to chains and collars. Thus, on all sides, they are impelled by an evil dæmon, to whom they have voluntarily surrendered themselves, by forsaking the eternal and saviour gods.

Statues and altars, and the preservation of the unextinguished fire, and, in short, all such particulars, have been established by our fathers as symbols of the presence of the gods; not that we should believe that these symbols are gods, but that through these we should worship the gods. For since we are connected with body, it is also necessary that our worship of the gods should be performed in a corporeal manner; but they are incorporeal. And they, indeed, have exhibited to us as the first of statues, that which ranks as the second genus of gods from the first, and which circularly revolves round the whole of heaven. Since, however, a corporeal worship cannot even be paid to these, because

---

* i.e. The Cappadocian monks and hermits.

they are naturally unindigent, a third kind of statues was devised in the earth, by the worship of which we render the gods propitious to us. For as those who reverence the images of kings, who are not in want of any such reverence, at the same time attract to themselves their benevolence; thus, also, those who venerate the statues of the gods, who are not in want of any thing, persuade the gods by this veneration to assist and be favourable to them. For alacrity in the performance of things in our power is a document of true sanctity; and it is very evident that he who accomplishes the former, will, in a greater degree, possess the latter. But he who despises things in his power, and afterwards pretends to desire impossibilities, evidently does not pursue the latter, but overlooks the former. For though divinity is not in want of any thing, it does not follow that on this account nothing is to be offered to him. For neither is he in want of celebration through the ministry of words. What then? Is it, therefore, reasonable that he should also be deprived of this? By no means. Neither, therefore, is he to be deprived of the honour which is paid him through works; which honour has been legally established, not for three, or for three thousand years, but in all preceding ages, among all nations of the earth.

But [the Galilæans will say], O! you who have admitted into your soul every multitude of dæmons, who though, according to you, they are formless and unfigured, you have fashioned in a corporeal resemblance, it is not fit that honour should be paid to divinity through such works. How, then, do we not consider as wood and stones those statues which are fashioned by the hands of men? O more stupid than even stones themselves! Do you fancy that all men are to be drawn by the nose as you are drawn by execrable dæmons, so as to think that the artificial resemblances of the gods are the gods themselves? Looking, therefore, to the resemblances of the gods, we do not think them to be either stones or wood; for neither do we think that the gods are these resemblances; since neither do we say that royal images are wood, or stone, or brass, nor that they are the kings themselves, but the images of kings. Whoever, therefore, loves his king, beholds with pleasure the image of his king; whoever loves his child is delighted with his image; and whoever loves his father surveys his image with delight. Hence, also, he who is a lover of divinity gladly surveys the statues and images of the gods; at the same time venerating and fearing with a holy dread the gods who invisibly behold him.[*] If, therefore, some one should fancy that these ought never

---

[*] The catholics have employed similar arguments in defence of the reverence which they pay to the images of the men whom they call saints. But the intelligent reader need not be told, that it is one thing to venerate the images of those divine powers which proceed from the great first cause of all things, and eternally subsist concentrated and rooted in him, and another to reverence the images of men who, when living, were the disgrace of human nature. In addition to what is said by Julian on this subject, the following extract from the treatise of Sallust, on the Gods and the World, is well worthy the attentive perusal of the] reader. "A divine nature is not indigent of any thing; but the honours which we pay to the gods are performed for the sake of our advantage. And since the providence of the gods is everywhere extended, a certain habitude, or fitness, is all that is requisite, in order to receive their beneficent communications. But all habitude is produced through imitation and similitude. Hence temples imitate the heavens, but altars the earth; statues resemble life, and on this account they are similar to animals. Prayers imitate that which is intellectual; but characters superior ineffable powers. Herbs and stones resemble matter; and animals which are sacrificed, the irrational life of our souls. But, from all these, nothing happens to the gods beyond what they already possess; for what accession can be made to a divine nature? But a conjunction with our souls and the gods is by these means produced.

to be corrupted, because they were once called the images of the gods, such a one appears to me to be perfectly void of intellect. For if this were admitted, it is also requisite that they should not be made by men. That, however, which is produced by a wise and good man may be corrupted by a depraved and ignorant man. But the gods which circularly revolve about the heavens, and which are living statues, fashioned by the gods themselves as resemblances of their unapparent essence, —these remain forever. No one, therefore, should disbelieve in the gods, in consequence of seeing and hearing that some persons have behaved insolently towards statues and temples. For have there not been many who have destroyed good men, such as Socrates and Dion, and the great Empedotimus? And who, I well know, have, more than statues or temples, been taken care of by the gods. See, however, that the gods knowing the body of these to be corruptible, have granted that it should yield and be subservient to nature; but afterwards have punished those by whom it was destroyed; which clearly happened to be the case with all the sacrilegious of our time.

Let no one, therefore, deceive us by words, nor disturb us with respect to providential interference. For as to the prophets of the Jews, who reproach us with things of this kind, what will they say of their own temple, which has been thrice destroyed, but has not been since, even to the present time, rebuilt? I do not, however, say this as reproaching them; for I have thought of rebuilding it, after so long a period, in honour of the divinity who is invoked in it. But I have mentioned this, being willing to show, that it is not possible for any thing human to be incorruptible; and that the prophets who wrote things of this kind were delirious, and the associates of stupid old women. Nothing, however, hinders, I think, but that God may be great, and yet he may not have worthy interpreters [of his will]. But this is because they have not delivered their soul to be purified by the liberal disciplines; nor their eyes, which are profoundly closed, to be opened; nor the darkness which oppresses them to be purged away. Hence, like men who survey a great light through thick darkness, neither purely nor genuinely, and in consequence of this do not conceive it to be a pure light, but a fire, and likewise perceiving nothing of all that surrounds it, but loudly exclaim, *Be seized with horror, be afraid, fire, flame, death, a knife, a two-edged sword,* expressing by many names the one noxious power of fire. Of these men, however, it is better peculiarly to observe how much inferior their teachers of the words of God are to our poets.

EPISTLE XLII.

AN EDICT, FORBIDDING THE CHRISTIANS TO TEACH THE LITERATURE OF THE HEATHENS.

WE are of opinion that proper erudition consists not in words, nor in elegant and magnificent language, but in the sane disposition of an intelligent soul, and in true opinions of good and evil, and of what is beautiful and base. Whoever, therefore, thinks one thing, and teaches another to his followers, appears to be no less destitute of erudition than he is of virtue. Even in trifles, if the mind and tongue be at variance, there is some kind of improbity. But in affairs of the greatest consequence, if a man thinks one thing, and teaches another contrary to what he thinks, in what respect does this differ from the conduct of those mean-spirited, dishonest, and abandoned traders, who generally affirm what they know to be false, in order to deceive and inveigle customers?

All, therefore, who profess to teach, ought to possess worthy manners, and should never entertain opinions opposite to those of the public; but such especially, I think, ought to be those who instruct youth, and explain to them the works of the ancients, whether they are orators or grammarians; but particularly if they are sophists. For these last affect to be the teachers, not only of words, but of manners, and assert that political philosophy is their peculiar province. Whether, therefore, this be true or not, I shall not at present consider. I commend those who make such specious promises, and should commend them much more if they did not falsify and contradict themselves by thinking one thing, and teaching their scholars another. What then? Were not Homer, Hesiod, Demosthenes, Herodotus, Thucydides, Isocrates, and Lysias, the leaders of all erudition? And did not some of them consider themselves sacred to Mercury, but others to the Muses? I think, there fore, it is absurd for those who explain their works to despise the gods whom they honoured.

I do not mean (for I think it would be absurd) that they should change their opinions for the sake of instructing youth; but I give them their option, either not to teach what they do not approve, or, if they choose to teach, first to persuade their scholars that neither Homer, nor Hesiod, nor any of those whom they expound and charge with impiety, madness, and error concerning the gods, are really such as they represent them to be. For as they receive a stipend, and are maintained by their works, if they can act with such duplicity for a few drachms, they confess themselves guilty of the most sordid avarice.

Hitherto, indeed, many causes have prevented their resorting to the temples; and the dangers that everywhere impended were a plea for concealing the most true opinions of the gods. But now, since the gods have granted us liberty, it seems to me absurd for any to teach those things to men which they do not approve. And if they think that those writers whom they expound, and of whom they sit as interpreters, are wise, let them first zealously imitate their piety towards the gods. But if they think they have erred in their conceptions of the most honourable natures [the gods], let them go into the churches of the Galilæans, and there expound Matthew and Luke, by whom being persuaded you forbid sacrifices. I wish that your ears and your tongues were (as you express it) regenerated in those things of which I wish that myself, and all who in thought and deed are my friends, may always be partakers.

To masters and teachers let this be a common law. But let no youths be prevented from resorting to whatever schools they please. It would be as unreasonable to exclude children, who know not yet what road to take, from the right path, as it would be to lead them by fear and with reluctance to the religious rites of their country. And though it would be just to cure such reluctance, like madness, even by force, yet let all be indulged with that disease. For I think it is requisite to instruct, and not to punish the ignorant.

Julian was certainly right in forbidding the Christians to teach the literature of the heathens; for *what business have those with such literature, who profess a religion by which it is despised? The study, therefore, of heathen writers by those who call themselves Christians, is nothing more than duplicity;* and that Pope who formed the design of destroying all the writings of the heathens, was certainly a consistent Christian, though a most execrable barbarian. He deserves to be ranked among the first of the saints, but was at least upon a level with the greatest savage!

That the reader, however, may be fully convinced that human learning is despised both by the founder of the Christian religion and his apostles, let him attend to the following testimonies from the scriptures themselves.

And, first, let us hear what Paul says, whom Julian calls the greatest of impostors: "I speak as a fool, I am more."[*] And again, "Take me as a fool." And, further, "I speak it not after the Lord, but as it were foolishly." And, in another place, "We are fools for Christ's sake." Again, "If any one among you

-----

[*] i.e. I am a knave. For it is very possible for a man to be a knave, and yet a fool in things of the greatest consequence.

seem to be wise, let him be a fool, that he may be wise." Farther, still, "God hath chosen the foolish things of this world." And "It pleased God, by foolishness to save the world." God himself, also, is made to say, by the mouth of his prophet, "I will destroy the wisdom of the wise, and cast away the understanding of the prudent." And Christ gives him thanks that he had concealed the mystery of salvation from the wise, but revealed it to babes and sucklings, that is to say, *fools;* for the Greek word for babes is *νηπιοι*, i.e. *fools*, which he opposes to the word *σοφοι*, i.e. *wise men.* In Luke, also, Jesus called those two disciples with whom he joined himself upon the way, fools. And, throughout the gospel, you find him ever accusing the scribes and pharisees, and doctors of the law, but diligently defending the ignorant multitude. For what else is the meaning of "Woe to ye scribes and pharisees!" than Woe to ye wise men? He, also, seems chiefly delighted with little children, women, and fishermen; carefully recommended folly to his apostles, but cautioned them against wisdom; and drew them together by the example of little children, lilies, mustard-seed, and sparrows, things senseless and inconsiderable, living only by the dictates of nature, and without either craft or care. To which we may add, that God forbade man to eat of the tree of knowledge, as if knowledge were the bane of happiness; and hence Paul disallows it, as puffing up and destructive. To all which we may further add, that in scripture there is frequent mention of harts, hinds, and lambs; and such as are destined to eternal life are called sheep, than which creature there is not any thing more foolish, if we may believe that proverb of Aristotle (*προβατειον ηθος*), *sheepish manners*, which he tells us is taken from the foolishness of that creature, and is usually applied to dull-headed people, and lack-wits. And yet Christ professes to be the shepherd of his flock, and is himself delighted with the name of a Lamb!

THE END.